MW00987532

Cooking with Trader Joe's®

The 5 inGReDienT COOKBOOK

Deana Gunn & wona Miniati

Cooking with Trader Joe's: The 5-Ingredient Cookbook
by Deana Gunn and Wona Miniati
Photographs by Deana Gunn and Wona Miniati
Designed by Lilla Hangay

Copyright © 2015 by Deana Gunn & Wona Miniati
Photographs copyright © 2015 by Deana Gunn & Wona Miniati

All rights reserved. Brown Bag Publishers and the Brown Bag Publishers logo are trademarks of Brown Bag Publishers, LLC. Other product and company names herein may be the trademarks of their respective owners. Rather than use a trademark symbol with every occurrence of a trademarked name, we are using the names only in an editorial fashion and to the benefit of the trademark owner, with no intention of infringement of the trademark.

No part of this book may be reproduced in whole or in part, or transmitted in any form or by any means, electronic or mechanical, including photocopying, recording, or by any information storage and retrieval system, without permission in writing from the publisher.

DISCLAIMER: The information in this book is not intended as medical advice or intended to cure, treat, or diagnose any ailment or disease. The authors, publishers, and/or distributors do not assume responsibility for any adverse consequences resulting form adopting any health information described herein.

Published by Brown Bag Publishers, LLC
PO. Box 235065
Encinitas, CA 92023

Printed in China

Library of Congress Cataloging-in-Publication Data
Gunn, Deana & Miniati, Wona.
Cooking with Trader Joe's: The 5 Ingredient Cookbook /
by Deana Gunn & Wona Miniati: photographs by Deana Gunn & Wona Miniati.-1st ed.
Includes index.

I. Quick and easy cookery. 2. Trader Joe's (Store) I. Title.

ISBN 978-1-938706-18-9

This book is an independent work not sponsored by or affiliated with Trader Joe's.
Trader Joe's is a registered trademark of Trader Joe's Company.

Table of Contents

Sides 167

Desserts & Drinks 189

Breakfast 233

Thank You Notes

A heartfelt thanks to our family and friends who continue to cheer us on as we enthusiastically create more cookbooks starring our favorite store.

We praise our talented designer Lilla Hangay for making each book more beautiful and fun than the one before. We also humbly thank our editor Heather World and our friend Shannon Callin for polishing our prose and helping us say all them thar words in the goodest way.

Many thanks to our customers who share their feedback and favorite recipes with us. We love hearing from you, and your kind emails and Facebook posts make our day. In fact, you are the inspiration behind this cookbook and why we are driven to keep creating recipes that make our lives easier and tastier.

A big shout-out to Trader Joe's, our favorite store in the whole wide world. We can't imagine a better place to shop or nicer crewmembers to greet us as we cruise the aisles.

We thank you all!

Introduction

Years ago, we had the idea to create something new: a Trader Joe's cookbook. It was the perfect way to share original recipes and cooking ideas that helped us create meals easily and quickly every night of the week.

The idea was simple: make Trader Joe's our one-stop shop and use their time-saving products in our recipes. For years, we had shopped the aisles, created recipes around what we saw, stocked up on our favorite products, and fantasized about how to use new products. We strategized about all the shortcuts that would cut our cooking time in a fraction of what it would be if we did everything the old-fashioned, from-scratch way. The cookbook was a resounding hit, because it turns out that we weren't the only ones looking for delicious, easy meals made in a snap.

Five ingredients or fewer

A piece of praise we hear repeatedly is how our ingredient lists are approachable and unintimidating: there isn't a long list of 24 ingredients requiring visits to multiple stores. The recipes are practical and doable, whether you're a busy cook or a novice cook, and the results are delicious.

In this new book, we pushed ourselves to create recipes with a limit of five ingredients. **Five!** **Salt, pepper, butter, and oil are freebies**; these pantry items are "grayed out" in the ingredient lists so that you can easily spot the (five or fewer) ingredients you'll need to shop for.

When shopping, prep work, and cooking take a fraction of the time as before, you really will have time to learn a new language, read a book, play board games with the kids, or throw the ball for the dog.

About our recipes and this book

Our recipes minimize ingredients but maximize taste. We have included:

1. Photos for every recipe.

We love cookbooks with photos. How else will you know if you'll like a recipe or what it will look like when it's done? We think it's necessary to have pictures with recipes, so we're continuing our tradition of giving you a photo of every single dish, made by us, in our own kitchens.

2. One-stop shopping at Trader Joe's.

We're too busy to run around from store to store, gathering ingredients. And we know you are too. The recipes in this book are built on one-stop shopping: get everything you need at Trader Joe's and then get ready for the easiest cooking you can imagine. Throughout the book, we've capitalized the names of unique Trader Joe's products, such as Fresh Bruschetta Sauce or Chunky Salsa. Of course, it's not a requirement to get everything at Trader Joe's, but it's a convenience we invite you to embrace. And yes, we recognize that occasionally an item will be out of stock or (heaven forbid!) discontinued. That's why we suggest substitutions in each recipe and keep a running list of substitutions on our website: **cookTJ.com**

3. Nutritional information.

You asked for it, and we listened. Nutritional data is given for every recipe so you can match menus to your dietary needs. Whether you're interested in carbs, calories, or fat, whether you follow popular diets or have your own regimen, we hope the nutritional data provided in this book will help you create healthy menus.

Nutritional analysis for recipes assumes 1% milk, unsalted butter, and low-fat yogurt unless otherwise noted. It does not include optional ingredients.

We note recipes that can be made vegetarian **or** gluten-free **using simple substitutions.**

Why Trader Joe's ?

We are always surprised when we run into someone who's never shopped at Trader Joe's, because we can't imagine life without it! Ask someone what they love most about Trader Joe's, and you'll likely hear some of these reasons:

- **Value and quality.** At Trader Joe's, you'll find everything from the very basics to high-end gourmet food at affordable prices. All the food is high quality and delicious, with organic and natural options found throughout the store.

- **Unique products.** Trader Joe's scouts the world for new and inspiring foods and beverages. Only those that pass Trader Joe's employee taste tests make it to stores.

- **Just food, no preservatives.** When you compare the labels on Trader Joe's products to items found at other stores, you'll notice something missing: a long list of chemicals, fillers, and preservatives.

- **No artificial flavors and no artificial colors.** Whether it's the "pink" in pink lemonade or the colorful candy coating on the Chocolate Sunflower Seed Drops, the colorings are natural (usually vegetable extracts) rather than synthetic food dyes. Flavorings are also natural, which not only taste better but are also healthier.

- **Nothing genetically engineered.** Trader Joe's was among the first national grocers to remove genetically modified food from its private label products.

- **Eco-conscious.** Trader Joe's is regularly recognized for its commitment to responsible buying practices. Trader Joe's brand eggs are cage-free. Hormone-free dairy products are the norm. Tuna is from "dolphin-safe" water (and as a result, low in mercury).

- **Wine and beer.** In addition to great food, Trader Joe's brings a wide and ever-evolving assortment of value-priced wines from all over the globe, including the famously nicknamed "Two-Buck Chuck." Trader Joe's international beer selection is second to none.

- **Fun-filled shopping experience.** Balloons, hand-written chalkboard signs, lively music, and cheerful crewmembers decked in Hawaiian flair create a friendly and casual atmosphere.

- **Gluten-free product listing.** Take a look at Trader Joe's website and you'll see a pretty comprehensive list of gluten-free products available at the store. As you shop, you will also see a gluten-free icon on many packages of Trader Joe's gluten-free products. Check labels because not all gluten-free products carry the icon.

So head on down to your nearest Trader Joe's with this cookbook in hand, and let us show you why this is our favorite grocer and our favorite way to cook.

1 Appetizers

Stovetop Spinach-Artichoke Dip

Hot and creamy spinach-artichoke dip is a party classic. Our version of this go-to appetizer is made quickly on the stovetop. It's easy, ready in minutes, and leaves the oven available for the main meal or dessert.

1 (16-oz) pkg frozen spinach, thawed

1 cup light or regular mayonnaise

1 (14-oz) can artichoke hearts, drained and chopped

1 cup shredded pepper jack cheese

2 cloves garlic, crushed, or 2 cubes frozen Crushed Garlic

1 tsp black pepper

1 Using hands, squeeze all water out of thawed spinach. It should measure 1 cup.

2 Combine all ingredients in a saucepan over medium heat and stir until cheese is melted and dip is very hot (2-3 minutes).

3 Serve immediately with crackers, pita chips, sliced baguette, or cut veggies.

Prep and cooking time: 10 minutes
Serves 8

Nutrition Snapshot

*Per serving: 120 calories, 6 g fat, 0 g saturated fat, 4 g protein,
9 g carbs, 2 g fiber, 3 g sugar, 248 mg sodium*

Vegetarian   Gluten Free

Zucchini Sticks

Zucchini bakes up tasty and crispy in the oven, without all the extra calories that come from deep frying. Breadcrumbs and Parmesan coat the zucchini, which is "oven-fried" at a high temperature. We won't pretend that these are the same as their deep-fried cousins, but they are gobbled up every time we make them. Serve the zucchini sticks with ranch-style dressing, hummus, marinara, or lemon aioli (lemon juice and garlic stirred into mayonnaise).

4 small zucchini or 2 medium zucchini

1 egg

½ cup breadcrumbs

⅓ cup finely grated Parmesan cheese

2 tsp 21 Seasoning Salute

¼ tsp salt

1 Preheat oven to 450° F.

2 Cut zucchini length-wise into ½-inch-thick spears and cut across to make 3-inch-long pieces.

3 Beat egg in a bowl. Add zucchini and toss to coat.

4 Combine breadcrumbs, Parmesan, and seasonings in another bowl. Press zucchini in breadcrumb mixture and coat each piece generously. Place on oiled baking sheet.

5 Bake for 10 minutes until zucchini are browned and crisp on edges. Flip and bake for additional 5 minutes. Sprinkle with a pinch of salt. Serve immediately.

Prep and cooking time: 25 minutes
Serves: 6

Nutrition Snapshot

Per serving: 87 calories, 2 g fat, 2 g saturated fat, 6 g protein, 12 g carbs, 1 g fiber, 3 g sugar, 277 mg sodium

Vegetarian Gluten Free

Substitute
almond meal for
breadcrumbs

Raspberry Baked Brie

Brie cheese baked in the oven transforms into a warm and creamy concoction that is always a hit at parties. Add sweet raspberry preserves and salted pecans to contrast the richness of Brie and to add texture. Triple sec deepens the flavor with a hint of orange. For other popular variations, substitute the same amounts of apricot jam and almonds, or pepper jelly and pepitas.

1 (~0.6-lb) wedge Brie cheese, such as Double Crème Brie

3 heaping Tbsp raspberry preserves, such as Organic Reduced Sugar Raspberry Preserves

3 Tbsp chopped roasted and salted pecans

1 Tbsp triple sec or Cointreau (optional)

1 Preheat oven to 400° F.

2 Cut off top rind of Brie. Place the wedge of Brie in a small baking dish that is slightly bigger than the Brie. Top with raspberry preserves and sprinkle with pecans. Drizzle with triple sec.

3 Cover tightly with foil and bake for 20-25 minutes (depends on size of Brie) or until cheese is melting and starting to ooze and fill the dish. Remove from oven and let dish cool slightly so no enthusiastic guest burns a hand or tongue. Serve with water crackers or crusty bread.

Prep time: 5 minutes
Hands-off cooking time: 20-25 minutes
Serves 6

Nutrition Snapshot
Per serving: 201 calories, 17 g fat, 10 g saturated fat,
8 g protein, 4 g carbs, 1 g fiber, 4 g sugar, 257 mg sodium

 Vegetarian
 Gluten Free

Hot Creamy Corn Dip

Trader Joe's Corn and Chile Salsa is a sweet and spicy tomato-less salsa. We use it to create this winning hot and creamy corn dip. The flavorful corn salsa gives it a subtle touch of heat, and Parmesan adds a savory cheesiness that rounds out the cream base. Green onion is added just before serving for a fresh crunch, color, and texture.

1 (13.75-oz) jar Corn and Chile Salsa

1 (8-oz) brick light or regular cream cheese, softened

½ cup sour cream

½ cup shredded Parmesan cheese

2 stalks green onion, chopped

1   Preheat oven to 350° F.

2   Add corn salsa, cream cheese, sour cream, and Parmesan to a bowl; stir until well combined. Transfer to oven-safe baking dish.

3   Bake for 25-30 minutes, until hot and edges are bubbly.

4   Sprinkle with green onion and serve with pita chips, corn chips, tortilla chips, or veggies.

Prep time: 5 minutes
Hands-off cooking time: 25-30 minutes
Serves 10

Nutrition Snapshot
Per serving: 147 calories, 7 g fat, 4 g saturated fat, 6 g protein, 14 g carbs, 1 g fiber, 9 g sugar, 254 mg sodium

Vegetarian   Gluten Free

Spicy Peanut Dip

Here is our version of the spicy peanut dip you may have tried in Thai or Indonesian restaurants. Trader Joe's Soyaki combines soy sauce with garlic, ginger, and sesame, balancing savory with a little bit of sweetness. Combine Soyaki with peanut butter and coconut milk with a touch of sesame oil for nutty smoothness. Sriracha hot sauce, made with chili peppers, gives it a little kick.

3 Tbsp Soyaki teriyaki sauce
¼ cup peanut butter
¼ cup canned light coconut milk
1 Tbsp toasted sesame oil
1 tsp Sriracha

1 Add all ingredients to a bowl; whisk until smooth, adding water to thin mixture if necessary.

2 Serve with veggies like baby carrots, bell peppers, and cucumber spears.

Prep time: 5 minutes
Serves 8

Nutrition Snapshot

Per serving: 83 calories, 7 g fat, 1 g saturated fat, 2 g protein, 4 g carbs, 1 g fiber, 0 g sugar, 196 mg sodium

  Substitute gluten-free teriyaki sauce, available at other grocers

Persian Eggplant Dip

Middle-Eastern-inspired eggplant dip takes minutes rather than hours, thanks to Trader Joe's Misto Alla Griglia, a combination of grilled eggplant and zucchini. The laborious prep and cooking of the eggplant is already done! Use a food processor to combine the ingredients into a smooth and savory dip. Serve alongside hummus and a tray of veggies, pita chips, or toasted flatbread.

1 (16-oz) pkg frozen Misto Alla Griglia, thawed

½ cup plain whole milk yogurt

2 cloves garlic, crushed, or 2 cubes frozen Crushed Garlic

¼ tsp salt

¼ tsp black pepper

Fresh mint for garnish (optional)

1   Combine Misto Alla Griglia, yogurt, garlic, salt, and pepper in a food processor and process until smooth (about 20-30 seconds). Garnish with chopped mint or sprig of mint.

Prep time: 10 minutes (not counting thawing)
Serves 6

Nutrition Snapshot

Per serving: 106 calories, 8 g fat, 1 g saturated fat,
2 g protein, 7 g carbs, 3 g fiber, 6 g sugar, 166 mg sodium

Tomato and Goat Cheese Flatbread Pizzas

Flatbread pizzas are the epitome of convenience – no messy dough and ready in no time. Cut into wedges, flatbread pizzas are a delicious hot appetizer that appeal to a range of tastes. Experiment with different toppings and have fun making an array of flatbread pizzas for your next get-together. If your oven is occupied by the main meal, make these tiny pizzas in your toaster oven.

2 Middle Eastern flatbread rounds

2 Tbsp refrigerated Genova Pesto

2 small tomatoes, very thinly sliced

2 Tbsp goat cheese

¼ cup chopped fresh basil

1 Preheat broiler on high setting. Set oven rack to center position.

2 Broil flatbreads for 1 minute or until golden. Remove from oven and flip, facing the toasted side down. Spread pesto on untoasted side of flatbreads, going all the way to the edges. Top with tomato slices and dot with goat cheese. Broil for 2-3 minutes, until edges of bread are golden brown.

3 Remove from oven and let cool for 1 minute. Sprinkle with basil. Cut into wedges and serve.

Prep time: 5 minutes
Hands-off cooking time: 3-4 minutes
Serves 4

Variation: Use fresh mozzarella instead of goat cheese. Fresh mozzarella (especially the kind packed in water) can get watery when cooked, leaving a puddle on your pizza. Avoid this by slicing and then pressing fresh mozzarella in between paper towels to soak up excess water.

Nutrition Snapshot
Per serving: 136 calories, 6 g fat, 2 g saturated fat, 4 g protein,
16 g carbs, 1 g fiber, 2 g sugar, 209 mg sodium

  Use brown rice tortillas and monitor closely to avoid burning

5-Minute Homemade Hummus

Homemade hummus takes just a few minutes to make, and store-bought hummus just can't compare in flavor. When serving, garnish with pine nuts or chopped parsley, a sprinkle of paprika, or a drizzle of olive oil. Serve hummus with pita triangles, pita chips, tortilla chips, in a falafel sandwich, or as a dip for just about any vegetable, such as carrots, cucumbers, or celery. We used a bell pepper as a playful (and edible) serving container.

2 (15-oz) cans garbanzo beans

2 cloves garlic, crushed, or 2 cubes frozen Crushed Garlic

½ tsp cumin

½ tsp salt

¼ cup extra virgin olive oil

Juice of 1 lemon (2 Tbsp lemon juice)

1   Drain one of the cans of beans. Add both cans (including the liquid of the second can) to a blender or food processor.

2   Add remaining ingredients and puree until hummus is smooth.

3   For best flavor, refrigerate for a few hours or overnight so flavors meld.

Prep time: 5 minutes
Serves 8

Nutrition Snapshot

Per serving: 150 calories, 7 g fat, 1 g saturated fat, 5 g protein, 17 g carbs, 5 g fiber, 1 g sugar, 486 mg sodium

Roasted Asparagus with Prosciutto

Roasting is one of the easiest ways to prepare asparagus. Take this stalky vegetable up a notch by wrapping the asparagus in a layer of crispy prosciutto, creating an elegant appetizer. Use asparagus that are at least ½-inch thick. Thin wispy spears will droop when cooked.

1 (12-oz) bag or bunch asparagus spears (about 12 spears), ends trimmed

2 tsp olive oil

¼ tsp black pepper

6 thin slices prosciutto (or half the number of asparagus spears)

1 Preheat broiler on high setting with rack on 2nd rung from top, about 6 inches below heating element.

2 Place asparagus on baking sheet and drizzle with oil. Season with pepper. Using hands, toss asparagus spears until they are evenly coated.

3 Wrap each asparagus spear with prosciutto, wrapping downward in a spiral. Place on baking sheet. Make sure spears do not touch each other, or the asparagus and prosciutto will steam instead of roast. The goal is crisp prosciutto.

4 Broil for 3 minutes, flip asparagus, and continue broiling about 2-3 minutes more.

Prep time: 10 minutes
Cooking time: 5 minutes
Serves 4

Nutrition Snapshot

Per serving: 85 calories, 5 g fat, 2 g saturated fat, 8 g protein, 3 g carbs, 2 g fiber, 2 g sugar, 360 mg sodium

G Gluten Free

Kale Chips

Turn fresh kale into a delicious good-for-you snack the whole family will enjoy! You can use any variety of kale, but curly kale is sweeter and more tender than flat kale. Use only enough oil to barely coat the leaves, or they will be soggy instead of crisp.

1 (10-oz bag) kale, stems removed

2 tsp olive oil

1 tsp Balsamic Glaze (optional)

¼ tsp salt

1   Preheat oven to 300° F. Line two rimmed baking sheets with parchment paper or silicone baking mats such as Silpat.

2   Whisk together oil and balsamic glaze. Drizzle over kale leaves. Using hands, rub oil into kale leaves until all leaves are lightly coated.

3   Arrange kale leaves in a single layer on baking sheet. Bake for 15 minutes, flip, and bake 15 minutes longer.

4   Let cool for 5 minutes before serving. Store in an airtight container for up to 1 week.

Note: The traditional way of making kale chips is to bake them at 350° F for 10-15 minutes. If you use this method, keep a close eye on the oven because even an extra 30 seconds can mean burnt kale chips. Baking at a lower temperature reduces the risk of burning.

Prep time: 10 minutes
Hand-off cooking time: 30 minutes
Serves 4

Variations: Try squeezing the juice of half a small lemon instead of Balsamic Glaze, or use ½ tsp soy sauce instead of salt. Add garlic powder, chili powder, or curry powder for extra kick and flavor.

Nutrition Snapshot

Per serving: 50 calories, 2 g fat, 0 g saturated fat, 2 g protein, 7 g carbs, 2 g fiber, 0 g sugar, 175 mg sodium

Smoked Trout Dip

Wona's friend Gloria Lee of Oakland, CA has a knack for throwing parties effortlessly, and the food is always outstanding. This sophisticated dip is one of Gloria's go-to party appetizers. Smoked trout is the highbrow cousin of other canned fish, worth being savored slowly. Don't let the can scare you: trout is much milder than other canned fish such as tuna or sardines, so don't shy away from this creamy lemony dip!

1 (3.9-oz) can smoked trout, drained

4 oz (½ a brick) light or regular cream cheese

2 heaping Tbsp Greek yogurt

Juice of ½ lemon (1 Tbsp lemon juice)

1 Tbsp chopped fresh chives or green onions

1   Add all ingredients to a bowl; stir until combined.

2   Serve with endive leaves, cucumber rounds, or thin crackers.

Prep time: 5 minutes
Serves 6

Nutrition Snapshot

*Per serving: 80 calories, 5 g fat, 2 g saturated fat,
7 g protein, 2 g carbs, 0 g fiber, 2 g sugar,
191 mg sodium*

G Gluten Free

Burrata and Bruschetta

How many times can you say burrata and bruschetta together without tripping over your tongue? Burrata, which means "buttered" in Italian, is a solid fresh mozzarella on the outside with a delightful filling of panna (cream). It goes beautifully with Trader Joe's Fresh Bruschetta Sauce, a fresh mixture of tomatoes, garlic, and basil. The burrata and bruschetta are layered on crostini, small pieces of toasted bread. This appetizer is ideal for large groups – simply lay out the ingredients and let guests assemble their own. We love drizzling Trader Joe's Balsamic Glaze on top for a fancy ultra-yummy touch.

1 (8-oz) container Burrata cheese

1 (12-oz) container refrigerated Fresh Bruschetta Sauce

Balsamic Glaze (optional)

1 baguette

2 Tbsp olive oil

1 Preheat oven to 350° F.

2 Slice baguette into thin slices. Brush or spray with oil. Bake for 10 minutes. Flip crostini and bake for another 5 minutes until evenly toasted.

3 To assemble, spread a slice of burrata cheese on crostini. Spoon bruschetta sauce on top, and drizzle with balsamic glaze.

Prep time: 10 minutes
Hands-off cooking time: 15 minutes
Serves 8

Nutrition Snapshot

Per serving: 265 calories, 16 g fat,
5 g saturated fat, 8 g protein, 17 g carbs,
1 g fiber, 3 g sugar, 451 mg sodium

Vegetarian   Gluten Free

Use gluten-
free bread

Roasted Artichokes

One of our favorite ways to prepare artichokes is to roast them in the oven to bring out a great nutty flavor. Be generous with the olive oil and balsamic vinegar. Ample seasoning is the secret to delicious artichokes!

4 large artichokes
4 cloves garlic, peeled
4 Tbsp balsamic vinegar
4 Tbsp olive oil
1 tsp salt

1 Preheat oven to 375° F.

2 Prepare artichokes by cutting off stems and top 1 inch of the leaves. Kitchen shears or scissors can be helpful for snipping the leaves.

3 Place a whole garlic clove in the center of each artichoke. You may need to create space by wriggling a knife in the center, or using your fingers. Drizzle each artichoke with 1 Tbsp balsamic vinegar and 1 Tbsp oil. Sprinkle with salt.

4 Wrap each artichoke individually in aluminum foil. Wrap tightly.

5 Place wrapped artichokes on a baking pan and bake for 50-60 minutes, or until artichoke bottoms are tender when pierced. Serve warm or at room temperature.

Prep time: 15 minutes
Hands-off cooking time: 50-60 minutes
Serves 4

Nutrition Snapshot
Per artichoke: 170 calories, 9 g fat, 1 g saturated fat,
5 g protein, 20 g carbs, 9 g fiber, 3 g sugar,
736 mg sodium

Vegetarian   Gluten Free

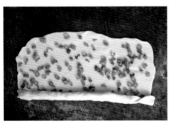   

Scallion Pancakes

Scallion pancakes are one of our favorite Chinese restaurant treats. Who can resist this flaky, chewy pan-fried bread? Wona learned to make these pancakes by watching a Chinese neighbor who speaks almost no English. You can make multiple batches and store pancakes in the freezer (cooked or uncooked), with layers of parchment paper in between to prevent sticking.

1 cup chopped scallions, green parts only

2 cups all-purpose flour, plus more for dusting

¾ cup hot water

½ tsp salt

1 Tbsp toasted sesame oil

1 Tbsp vegetable oil

1   Mix flour with water, kneading until a smooth dough forms. If dough is too dry, add more water, a spoonful at a time. Dough should be smooth and very elastic. Lift dough out of bowl, coat dough lightly in vegetable oil, and put back in bowl. Cover bowl with a damp cloth and let dough rest for 30 minutes, or up to overnight in fridge.

2   Divide dough into 4 equal parts. Lightly dust cutting board with flour and roll each portion of dough into a thin rectangle. Lightly brush dough with sesame oil and sprinkle evenly with scallions and salt. Starting from long end, roll dough up tightly, creating one long roll of scallion-filled dough. Repeat with remaining parts of dough.

3   Coil each roll into a round flat bundle. Place coil on cutting board and roll into a thin circle, using more flour to dust as needed. Repeat with remaining coils.

4   Heat a skillet or sauté pan over medium-high heat. Drizzle with vegetable oil and use a spatula to spread evenly. Cook pancakes 2 minutes on each side, or until golden brown.

5   To serve, cut pancakes into wedges and serve with soy sauce or a combination of soy sauce and rice wine vinegar.

Prep time: 20 minutes (not counting 30 minutes resting time)
Cooking time: 12 minutes
Makes 4 pancakes

Nutrition Snapshot

Per pancake: 296 calories, 8 g fat, 1 g saturated fat,
7 g protein, 50 g carbs, 2 g fiber, 1 g sugar, 296 mg sodium

Vegetarian

2 Soups & Salads

Tomato and Mozzarella Salad

This simple salad is a summer classic. It's perfect for warm days when ripe tomatoes and fresh basil are plentiful and you want delicious food that is quick to prepare and involves no cooking. The fresh ingredients are brought together with a simple balsamic vinaigrette. It's sophisticated enough for upscale gatherings and at the same time a favorite with kids. Deana's 12-year-old son Mason stood by with a fork in hand whenever she was testing or photographing this recipe.

2 cups halved cherry or grape tomatoes (about 10 oz of tomatoes)

1 (8-oz) container Ciliegine Fresh Mozzarella Balls, halved (about 1 ½ cups)

½ cup chopped fresh basil

2 tsp extra virgin olive oil

2 tsp balsamic vinegar

1 Add tomatoes, mozzarella balls, and basil to a bowl.

2 Whisk together oil and balsamic vinegar. Pour over salad, tossing gently to combine.

Prep time: 5-10 minutes
Serves 4 (or one 12-year-old boy)

Nutrition Snapshot

Per serving: 213 calories, 12 g fat, 6 g saturated fat, 20 g protein,
11 g carbs, 2 g fiber, 3 g sugar, 317 mg sodium

Helpful Tip: Trader Joe's sells large, healthy live basil plants for just a few dollars. It's a great deal, and, after you pinch off the leaves, you can plant it in your garden.

Raw Fennel Apple Salad

Raw fennel is sweet with a subtle anise flavor. It's also packed with phytonutrients, fiber, folate, potassium, anti-cancer components, and a multitude of vitamins. This healthy salad combines sliced fennel with apple, creating a delicious, sweet, crispy, and crunchy treat. A simple lemon-honey-yogurt vinaigrette pulls it together. Trader Joe's sells fresh fennel bulbs, two to a pack.

1 large bulb fennel

1 large, crisp apple such as Honeycrisp or Pink Lady

¼ cup plain whole milk yogurt

Juice of 1 lemon (2 Tbsp lemon juice)

1 Tbsp honey

⅛ tsp salt

¼ tsp black pepper

1 Slice fennel and apple thinly. Cut across slices to make bite-size pieces.

2 Add fennel and apple slices to a salad bowl. (If there are any leafy tops of the fennel, include those as well but discard the tough stalks.)

3 Whisk together yogurt, lemon juice, honey, salt, and pepper. Drizzle over salad and toss well.

Prep time: 10 minutes
Serves 4

Variation: Make an orange vinaigrette using ¼ cup yogurt, 2 Tbsp orange juice, and seasonings, but omit the honey.

Nutrition Snapshot
Per serving: 85 calories, 1 g fat, 0 g saturated fat, 2 g protein, 20 g carbs, 3 g fiber, 14 g sugar, 112 mg sodium

Vegetarian Gluten Free

Aloha Arugula Salad

Packages of combined papaya, pineapple, and mango slices are available in the refrigerated produce section of Trader Joe's, making it easy to add tropical flair to our favorite salad green. Peppery arugula is balanced perfectly with tangy lemon, savory Parmesan, and sweet tropical fruit. Mahalo!

1 (7-oz) bag arugula (about 5 cups)

1 (16-oz) container refrigerated Tropical Fruit Medley, diced (3 cups), or 3 cups diced mango

¼ cup fresh lemon juice

¼ cup extra virgin olive oil

¼ tsp salt

¼ tsp black pepper

½ cup shredded Parmesan cheese

1 Place arugula in a large salad bowl.

2 In a small bowl, whisk together lemon juice, oil, salt, and pepper. Pour dressing over arugula and toss to coat.

3 Add fruit and Parmesan, tossing gently to combine.

Prep time: 10 minutes
Serves 4

Nutrition Snapshot

Per serving: 228 calories, 17 g fat, 4 g saturated fat, 6 g protein, 16 g carbs, 2 g fiber, 11 g sugar, 329 mg sodium

Vegetarian   Gluten Free

Albondigas Soup

You dig soup! I dig soup! We all dig Albondigas soup! Albondigas soup is a traditional Mexican soup featuring meatballs in a flavorful broth of vegetables and herbs. It is delicious comfort food. We make a speedy version using pre-made mini meatballs. You can substitute other vegetables such as carrots, green beans, kale, or zucchini. Buen provecho!

2 trimmed leeks, or 1 large onion, chopped

1 Tbsp olive oil

1 (32-oz) carton beef broth

½ cup salsa of any kind, such as Salsa Verde or Chunky Salsa

Half (20-oz) pkg frozen Party Size Mini Meatballs

4 cups chopped Swiss chard or cabbage

1 Heat oil in a large pot over medium-high heat. Add leeks; cook and stir for 5 minutes until softened, stirring occasionally. Add 1-2 Tbsp of water if needed to speed softening of leeks. If using pre-sliced Frozen Leeks, no water is needed.

2 Add remaining ingredients and heat to boiling. Cover, reduce to low, and simmer for 30 minutes so flavors can meld. Serve immediately.

Prep time: 10 minutes   **Hands-off cooking time**: 35 minutes   **Serves** 6

Nutrition Snapshot

Per serving: 254 calories, 11 g fat, 4 g saturated fat,
10 g protein, 11 g carbs, 2 g fiber, 3 g sugar, 928 mg sodium

Use meatless meatballs and vegetarian broth

Use gluten-free broth

Thai Potsticker Soup

Potstickers, also known as gyoza, are savory Asian dumplings filled with chicken, pork, shrimp, or vegetables. Frozen potstickers are staples in our freezer, ready to be pan cooked, combined with stir-fried veggies, or used in a soup like we have here. Trader Joe's mouth-watering Thai Red Curry Sauce forms the base, thinned with savory chicken broth. Baby bok choy and basil add color and fresh flavor.

1 (1-lb) bag frozen potstickers, any variety

1 (11-oz) jar Thai Red Curry Sauce

3 cups low-sodium chicken broth

2 cups sliced baby bok choy (approximately 3 baby bok choy)

¼ cup chopped fresh basil

1 Add curry and broth to a saucepan over medium high heat. Stir together and bring to a simmer.

2 Add potstickers and bok choy, simmering for 10 minutes until potstickers are heated through. Stir in basil and serve.

Prep time: 2 minutes
Hands-off cooking time: 15 minutes
Serves 6

Nutrition Snapshot

Per serving: 180 calories, 7 g fat, 4 g saturated fat, 8 g protein, 20 g carbs, 3 g fiber, 3 g sugar, 1095 mg sodium

Vegetarian

Use vegetable potstickers and vegetable broth

BLT Panzanella

Panzanella is a Tuscan-born veggie salad with chewy bread cubes soaked with tasty salad dressing. We put a spin on the classic BLT (bacon, lettuce, and tomato) sandwich and dreamt it up as a panzanella, where the bread cubes soak up the tangy balsamic vinaigrette and the rich bacon drippings. Use leftover Italian or French bread, such as a stale baguette or boule, regular or sourdough. If making this salad in the summer, use it as great backdrop to showcase beautiful heirloom tomatoes.

8 oz uncooked bacon

5 cups shredded Romaine or butter lettuce

1 (1-lb) container heirloom cherry tomatoes, halved, or 4 tomatoes cut into wedges

Half a French baguette or boule, cut into 1-inch cubes (about 3-4 cups)

⅓ cup Balsamic Vinaigrette (use ready-made or recipe page 66)

1 Cook bacon in a large skillet until crisp and fat has rendered, about 15 minutes. Remove bacon and place on paper towels to drain. Set aside.

2 Pour out and reserve bacon grease; wipe skillet clean. To the same skillet, add back 1 Tbsp reserved bacon grease; add bread cubes, toss to coat, and cook over medium heat until bread is nicely toasted on all sides, about 3-5 minutes.

3 Chop or crumble bacon. Add bacon, lettuce, tomato, and bread to a salad bowl. Toss with dressing. Let salad sit for at least 10 minutes for bread to start soaking up dressing.

Note: Trader Joe's "Ends & Pieces" bacon works well here—use half the 16-oz package. If you're in a rush or don't feeling like cooking bacon, use ½ a package of Fully Cooked Bacon and crisp according to package instructions. Substitute olive oil for the bacon drippings.

Prep time: 10 minutes
Cooking time: 20 minutes (5 minutes if using Fully Cooked Bacon)
Serves 6

Nutrition Snapshot

Per serving: 208 calories, 12 g fat, 4 g saturated fat,
11 g protein, 17 g carbs, 2 g fiber, 4 g sugar, 744 mg sodium

Vegetarian
Use vegetarian bacon; substitute olive oil for bacon drippings.

Gluten Free
Use gluten-free bread

Tortellini Soup

Trader Joe's ready-made soups were born for add-ins like veggies and pasta. We took flavorful Roasted Pepper and Tomato Soup and made it more hearty by adding fresh tortellini and baby spinach. Creamy crème fraiche and crunchy chives top the rich soup.

1 (32-oz) carton Roasted Pepper and Tomato Soup

1 (10-oz) pkg refrigerated cheese tortellini

3 oz (½ bag) baby spinach

4 Tbsp crème fraiche

¼ cup chopped fresh chives

1 Pour soup into a medium saucepan and bring to a simmer over medium heat.

2 Add tortellini and cook 6 minutes.

3 Add baby spinach and cook an additional 3 minutes. If using large-leaf spinach, chop into smaller pieces. There is no need to chop baby spinach as it wilts down quite a bit.

4 When serving, top each bowl with 1 Tbsp crème fraiche and garnish with 1 Tbsp chives.

Prep time: 5 minutes
Hands-off cooking time: 12 minutes
Serves 4

Nutrition Snapshot

Per serving: 363 calories, 12 g fat, 8 g saturated fat, 16 g protein, 50 g carbs, 4 g fiber, 12 g sugar, 968 mg sodium

Vegetarian

Citrus Kale Salad

Fresh kale is brightened up with a lemony vinaigrette and orange segments, topped with crunchy pepitas (toasted pumpkin seeds). With the addition of dressing, kale will soften and become slightly translucent but will not wilt like other salad greens. Leftover salad can still be enjoyed later that day or even the next day.

1 (10-oz) bag kale (curly kale, dinosaur kale, or other thick kale)

1 (11-oz) can mandarin orange segments (drain but reserve 2 Tbsp syrup)

¼ cup fresh lemon juice

¼ cup extra virgin olive oil

¼ tsp salt

¼ tsp freshly ground black pepper

¼ cup toasted pepitas (pumpkin seeds)

1   Place kale on working surface. Remove any tough stems from the kale leaves and then chop the kale into smaller ribbons. Add kale to a large salad bowl.

2   In a small bowl, whisk together lemon juice, oil, 2 Tbsp syrup from mandarin orange can, salt and pepper. Pour dressing over the kale, tossing it with tongs to make sure it is coated thoroughly. Add drained mandarin segments and pepitas right before serving so that pepitas stay crunchy.

Prep time: 10 minutes
Serves 6

Nutrition Snapshot
Per serving: 172 calories, 12 g fat, 2 g saturated fat, 3 g protein,
16 g carbs, 2 g fiber, 9 g sugar, 132 mg sodium

Vegetarian   Gluten Free

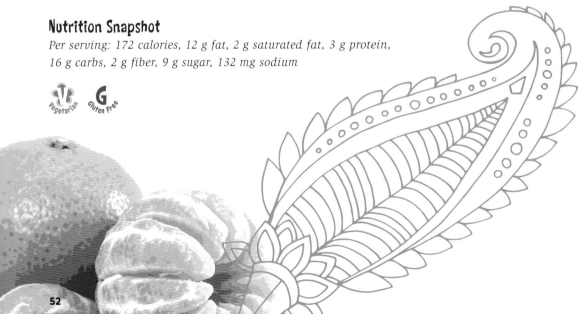

French Onion Soup

Mais oui! French onion soup is simpler and easier than you dreamed. Rich brown soup, toasted bread crouton on top, cheese melting on top and down the sides. It's très easy but it does take some time to properly cook and caramelize the onions. The longer you cook, the better the broth. Trader Joe's has a shredded Swiss & Gruyère cheese blend that was simply destined for this recipe.

3 jumbo yellow onions, sliced ¼-inch thick (about 1.5 lbs of onion)

2 Tbsp butter

2 Tbsp olive oil

¼ tsp salt

½ tsp black pepper

1 (32-oz) carton beef broth

¼ cup red wine (or use ¼ cup sherry for more traditional flavor)

6 slices sourdough boule or baguette

2 cups shredded Swiss & Gruyère cheese blend

1   Add butter and oil to a large pot over medium-high heat. When butter has melted, add onion, salt, and pepper and sauté over medium heat for 30 minutes until onions are well caramelized and brown. Add a generous pinch of sugar to speed caramelization.

2   Add broth and wine; bring to a boil, then reduce heat and simmer covered for 15 minutes.

3   Preheat broiler and place rack on center rung.

4   Toast bread on both sides under broiler or in toaster.

5   Divide soup into 6 bowls and top each with one slice of toasted bread. Sprinkle with cheese, dividing the cheese between the bowls

6   Place bowls on a baking sheet and place under broiler for 2 minutes or until cheese is melted and bubbly.

7   Wait one or two minutes before serving to let rims of bowls cool enough to handle.

Prep time: 5 minutes
Cooking time: 45-50 minutes (mostly hands off)
Serves 6

Nutrition Snapshot

Per serving: 295 calories, 20 g fat, 10 g saturated fat,
14 g protein, 18 g carbs, 1 g fiber, 4 g sugar, 597 mg sodium

Use vegetable broth

Use gluten-free bread and gluten-free broth

Pretty in Pink Salad

Trader Joe's ready-to-use Steamed & Peeled Baby Beets are a fabulous shortcut. Grab these pre-cooked packaged beets from the refrigerated produce section, and save yourself the time and stain-potential of peeling and cooking beets. The pink dressing is enhanced with the red juice from the beets, making a delightfully colorful salad. The tart-sweet flavors of cranberry, walnut, and gorgonzola in the ready-made dressing pair well with the sweetness of the beets.

1 (7-oz) pkg Butter Lettuce

1 (8-oz) pkg refrigerated Steamed & Peeled Baby Beets, diced

⅓ cup refrigerated Cranberry, Walnut & Gorgonzola Dressing

1 (1.75-oz) pkg Microgreens

1   Add lettuce and beets to a large salad bowl. Drizzle with dressing and toss to combine.

2   Top with microgreens and serve.

Prep time: 5 minutes
Serves 4

Nutrition Snapshot

Per serving: 125 calories, 5 g fat, 0 g saturated fat, 3 g protein,
16 g carbs, 2 g fiber, 12 g sugar, 25 mg sodium

Lemony Lentil Soup

Ready-to-use steamed lentils make this soup a snap. Leeks add great flavor to soups, and we love how their silky, subtle taste complements earthy lentils. Parsley and lemon juice make the soup fresh and bright, and balance out the subtle sweetness of cooked leeks. Trader Joe's sells trimmed leeks (just the white and light green part that is cleaned and ready to use) but feel free to use the whole leek if you have it—just wash the dark outer leaves carefully as they can collect soil.

1 (17.6-oz) pkg refrigerated Steamed Lentils

1 Tbsp olive oil

2 trimmed leeks, chopped (about 3-4 cups)

3 cups chicken broth

Juice of 1 lemon (2 Tbsp lemon juice)

½ cup chopped fresh parsley

1 Add oil to a saucepan or pot over medium heat. Add leeks; cook and stir for 8 minutes or until leeks are very soft, occasionally adding water a tablespoon at a time to keep leeks moist and to speed cooking.

2 Add broth and lentils and stir together. Bring to a boil, reduce heat, cover, and simmer for 10 minutes. Stir in lemon juice and parsley right before serving.

Prep time: 5 minutes
Cooking time: 20 minutes
Serves 4

Nutrition Snapshot
Per serving: 224 calories, 4 g fat, 1 g saturated fat,
14 g protein, 33 g carbs, 11 g fiber, 5 g sugar, 723 mg sodium

Tip: Use low-sodium broth to reduce sodium by over half.

Use vegetable broth

Use gluten-free chicken broth

Gingered Edamame Salad

This colorful salad starts with pre-cooked and shelled edamame. Pair with packaged shredded carrots to add vitamins, crunch, and vibrant color. Stop there or add what's left in the crisper: sliced bell peppers, shredded cabbage, chopped broccoli, or any other veggies you have on hand. Snappy sesame ginger dressing makes it all come together effortlessly.

1 (9-oz) pkg shelled edamame
Half (10-oz) pkg Shredded Carrots
1 cup cashews
⅓ cup Sesame Soy Ginger Vinaigrette

1   Roughly chop carrots to cut some of the really long carrot shreds.

2   Combine all ingredients in a bowl and toss to coat evenly.

Prep time: 5 minutes
Serves 6

Nutrition Snapshot

Per serving: 199 calories, 11 g fat, 2 g saturated fat,
8 g protein, 17 g carbs, 4 g fiber, 7 g sugar, 345 mg sodium

Creamy Curried Shrimp Soup

Tender shrimp and roasted corn are combined in a creamy curry base. Trader Joe's roasted corn is quick and convenient, capturing the flavor of char-grilled fresh corn any time of year. Using ready-made soup, curry sauce, and cooked shrimp makes this flavorful soup ready in minutes, taking only the time to heat the ingredients. Add fresh cilantro, or substitute basil if you don't like cilantro.

1 (32-oz) carton Creamy Corn and Roasted Pepper Soup

1 (16-oz) bag frozen Roasted Corn

½ cup jarred Thai Red Curry Sauce

1 (1-lb) bag frozen large cooked shrimp (peeled and tail off)

¼ cup chopped fresh cilantro

1 Combine soup, corn, curry, and shrimp in medium saucepan. There is no need to thaw any of the ingredients. Bring to a simmer and turn heat to low; let simmer for 5 minutes until soup is heated through.

2 Stir in cilantro.

Prep and cooking time: 10 minutes
Serves 8

Nutrition Snapshot

Per serving: 194 calories, 4 g fat, 1 g saturated fat, 15 g protein, 25 g carbs, 4 g fiber, 11 g sugar, 825 mg sodium

Omit shrimp
or substitute
tofu cubes

Garlic Parmesan Croutons

Croutons dress up any salad or soup with crunch and flavor. Moreover, they're the perfect use for stale or leftover baguettes, sandwich bread, or even bagels. We suggest collecting and dicing leftover pieces of bread and storing them in the freezer so you always have a supply on hand to make croutons. They'll go fast!

4 cups diced bread (leftover baguettes work well)

3 Tbsp olive oil or melted butter

3 Tbsp grated Parmesan cheese

½ tsp garlic powder

Pinch black pepper

1 Preheat oven to 350° F.

2 Drizzle bread with oil and toss until well combined. Sprinkle with Parmesan, garlic, and pepper; toss again.

3 Line a baking sheet with a Silpat mat or parchment paper. Spread out croutons in a single layer.

4 Bake for 15 minutes or until browned. Let cool. Store croutons in a covered container at room temperature.

Prep time: 5 minutes
Hands-off cooking time: 15 minutes
Serves 8

Nutrition Snapshot

Per serving: 99 calories, 6 g fat, 1 g saturated fat, 2 g protein,
9 g carbs, 0 g fiber, 2 g sugar, 153 mg sodium

Use gluten-
free bread

Homemade Vinaigrette

Once you get in the habit of making your own vinaigrette, you'll wonder why it ever seemed hard to make. It takes only a few minutes, you can adjust ingredients to your liking, and it can be made in batches for the whole week. We like adding mustard. Not only does it add flavor, it also helps the dressing emulsify, binding the oil and vinegar together. The sweetness of honey balances the mustard and vinegar. Use vinaigrette for salads, to marinate grilled meats and vegetables, or even as a dipping sauce for warm bread.

⅓ cup vinegar, such as Muscat Orange
    Champagne Vinegar or balsamic vinegar
2 tsp Hot & Sweet Mustard (or 1 tsp honey or
    sugar + 1 tsp Dijon mustard)
1 garlic clove, crushed, or 1 cube frozen
    Crushed Garlic
½ cup olive oil
¼ tsp salt
Pinch black pepper

1   Add all ingredients to a bowl; whisk until smooth. Taste and adjust seasonings.

2   If not using dressing right away, cover and refrigerate. Whisk again before use.

Prep time: 5 minutes
Makes 14 1-Tbsp servings

Nutrition Snapshot

*Per tablespoon: 78 calories, 8 g fat,
1 g saturated fat, 0 g protein, 0 g carbs,
0 g fiber, 2 g sugar, 47 mg sodium*

Asian Cucumber Salad

This refreshing salad features our favorite cucumbers, thin-skinned Persian cucumbers that are small, crisp, and sweet. Chef and cooking instructor Judith Sarchielli in Southern California sent us this recipe for a versatile salad that pairs nicely with any Asian-themed meal. For extra flavor, drizzle a little toasted sesame oil on top. Add black sesame seeds if you have them on hand. They look terrific contrasted against the light cucumbers.

5-6 small Persian cucumbers, thinly sliced in rounds
½ small red onion, thinly sliced
1 tsp sugar
2 Tbsp seasoned rice vinegar
1 tsp sesame seeds
½ tsp salt

1 Combine all ingredients in a bowl and toss to coat.

2 Chill for an hour. Keeps for a week refrigerated.

Prep time: 10 minutes
Serves 4

Variations: Use an 8-oz bag of trimmed radishes, thinly sliced in rounds, in place of the onions. For extra spice, sprinkle a pinch or two of crushed red pepper flakes.

Nutrition Snapshot
Per serving: 36 calories, 0 g fat, 0 g saturated fat, 2 g protein, 8 g carbs, 3 g fiber, 2 g sugar, 297 mg sodium

3 Main Meals

Broiled Middle-Eastern Lemon Chicken

Lemon and yogurt have been combined in marinades for centuries, resulting in deliciously juicy chicken. We use the broiler to get an effect similar to grilling, sealing in the flavors and slightly caramelizing edges on the outside. Serve with our Dill Rice (page 176). The marinade is very versatile – use it for kabobs or whole pieces of chicken, boneless or bone-in.

1.5-2 lb boneless skinless chicken thighs, cut into 3 or 4 smaller pieces.

½ cup plain whole milk yogurt

Juice of 1 lemon (2 Tbsp lemon juice)

1 Tbsp olive oil

1 tsp salt

½ tsp black pepper

½ medium onion, sliced thinly

1 Whisk together yogurt, lemon, oil, salt, and pepper. Stir in chicken and onion. Marinate chicken for 1 hour or up to 24 hours.

2 Preheat broiler and place rack on second rung from top (6 inches below broiler).

3 Place chicken pieces on lightly oiled broiling pan. Discard used marinade.

4 Broil 5 minutes one side, flip, and broil 5 more minutes or until done.

Prep and cooking time: 20 minutes (not including time to marinate)
Serves 6

Nutrition Snapshot
Per serving: 110 calories, 5 g fat, 1 g saturated fat,
14 g protein, 1 g carbs, 0 g fiber, 1 g sugar, 161 mg sodium

Mediterranean Couscous

Israeli couscous, also known as "pearl couscous" is a made of small toasted balls of semolina and wheat flour. Israeli couscous is larger than regular couscous, with a chewy texture and a nutty flavor. While it is bland on its own, it mixes beautifully with all sorts of Mediterranean additions like sun-dried tomato, basil, olives, and pine nuts. For a heartier meal, add other ingredients such as cooked chicken, sausage, or feta cheese.

1 (8-oz) pkg Israeli couscous (about 1⅔ cups)

⅓ cup jarred Julienne Sliced Sun Dried Tomato

⅓ cup chopped fresh basil

½ cup pitted kalamata olives, drained and chopped

⅓ cup pine nuts

¼ tsp salt

¼ tsp black pepper

1   Measure out 1 Tbsp of oil from the jar of sun-dried tomatoes and add to a saucepan over medium heat. Add couscous and stir 1-2 minutes until couscous is lightly browned and toasted.

2   Add 2 cups water and bring to a boil. Turn heat to low and simmer covered for 12 minutes or until liquid is absorbed. Stir in sun-dried tomato, chopped basil, olives, and pine nuts. Season with salt and pepper.

Prep time: 5-10 minutes
Cooking time: 14 minutes (mostly hands off)
Serves 6

Nutrition Snapshot
Per serving: 265 calories, 12 g fat, 1 g saturated fat,
6 g protein, 32 g carbs, 1 g fiber, 2 g sugar, 436 mg sodium

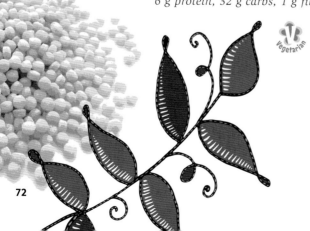

Chimichurri Stuffed Red Peppers

Stuffed bell peppers look time consuming to make, but they don't have to be. Here we fill bell pepper halves with Trader Joe's flavorful chimichurri rice and spicy soy chorizo, creating a complete meal in an edible vessel. Yum! We use the microwave in this quick and easy recipe, which is especially nice in the hot summer months or when you want to have dinner ready in 10 minutes.

2 large red bell peppers (or 4 small bell peppers)
1 (12-oz) bag frozen Chimichurri Rice or frozen Multigrain Blend with Vegetables
½ (12-oz) pkg Soy Chorizo or 2 sausages of your choice, diced
½ cup Shredded 3 Cheese Blend

1 Thaw Chimichurri Rice overnight in fridge. or warm according to package instructions. It can be cool or warm, as long as it's not frozen.

2 Cut bell peppers in half (stem to end) and clean out seeds and membranes. If using small peppers, cut the tops off and use each pepper whole.

3 Place pepper halves on microwave-safe dish, cover with plastic wrap, and microwave for 4 minutes. This step will blanch/soften the peppers and prepare them for filling. Be careful when removing from microwave as peppers will be steaming.

4 Combine rice and soy chorizo in a bowl, mixing until well combined. Divide mixture among the four pepper halves. Cover again with plastic wrap and return to microwave for 6 minutes. Top with cheese, cover loosely, and microwave 1 more minute to melt cheese.

Note: This entire dish can be cooked in the microwave. If you prefer to bake in the oven, stuff raw peppers, top with cheese, and bake uncovered at 350° F for about 35-40 minutes.

Prep time: 5-10 minutes
Hands-off cooking time: 11 minutes using microwave, 40 minutes using oven

Nutrition Snapshot

Per serving: 294 calories, 16 g fat,
6 g saturated fat, 13 g protein, 28 g carbs,
6 g fiber, 10 g sugar, 1222 mg sodium

Wasabi Chive Egg Salad

Trader Joe's Wasabi Mayonnaise gives traditional egg salad a nice kick. Deana's kids love this basic egg salad recipe. They love the wasabi, but if you want to make a mild version, just use regular mayonnaise. Serve with bread or on a bed of Romaine lettuce.

8 hardboiled eggs, peeled (sold at TJ's pre-cooked, or boil your own)

¼ cup chopped celery (1 stalk)

1 pickle, chopped or ¼ cup chopped pickle

2 Tbsp finely chopped fresh chives

¼ cup Wasabi Mayonnaise (2-3 Tbsp for a drier egg salad)

⅛ tsp salt

⅛ tsp black pepper

1 Chop eggs and add to a medium bowl. Add celery, pickle, and chives.

2 Add mayonnaise and stir until just combined. Season with salt and pepper.

Prep time: 10 minutes if using already boiled eggs
Serves 4

Nutrition Snapshot
Per serving: 248 calories, 21 g fat, 4 g saturated fat, 13 g protein,
1 g carbs, 0 g fiber, 1 g sugar, 287 mg sodium

Use gluten-free bread
or serve on romaine
leaves

Seared Scallops with Spuds and Greens

The secret to beautifully cooked scallops is a hot pan and dry scallops. We combine oil and butter in a very hot pan, making sure to pat scallops dry before seasoning them. Scallops require minimal cooking – overcook them and you've transformed these tender morsels into rubber pucks. We serve them with a small portion of potatoes, vibrant seasoned kale, and a drizzle of delicious lemon-cream sauce.

1 (1-lb) bag scallops (about 15-18 medium size scallops), thawed if frozen
½ (16-oz) bag Frozen Mashed Potatoes
1 bag kale or baby spinach
2 Tbsp olive oil, divided
2 Tbsp butter, divided
½ tsp salt, divided
½ tsp black pepper, divided
½ cup heavy cream
Juice of 1 lemon (2 Tbsp lemon juice)

1   Heat mashed potatoes according to package instructions. Set aside.

2   Place kale in wide saucepan with 1 Tbsp oil and 1 Tbsp butter over medium-low heat. Sprinkle with ¼ tsp each salt and pepper and add ½ cup water. Use tongs to toss in pan until kale is coated with oils and water. Cover pan and cook 3-5 minutes until kale is wilted. Remove from heat and set aside.

3   Rinse scallops in cold water and pat dry. Season with remaining salt and pepper. In pan over high heat, add remaining 1 Tbsp oil and 1 Tbsp butter. When pan is very hot, add scallops and make sure they are not touching each other. Sear scallops 90 seconds first side, flip, and cook 60 seconds on other side or until scallops are opaque. Do not overcook.

4   Remove scallops from pan. Remove pan from heat and immediately add cream and lemon to the browned butter in pan, stirring for 2 minutes until hot and slightly thickened. Residual heat from the hot pan should be enough to heat and thicken sauce.

5   Divide mashed potatoes among 4 plates. Top with kale, drizzle with cream sauce, and divide scallops. Serve immediately.

Prep and cooking time: 15 minutes
Serves 4

Nutrition Snapshot

Per serving: 336 calories, 19 g fat, 9 g saturated fat, 12 g protein, 31 g carbs, 1 g fiber, 1 g sugar, 736 mg sodium

Slow Cooker Salsa Chicken

The slow cooker is an important tool in the cook's arsenal of short cuts. It slaves away all day just so we can come home to a warm and waiting dinner. It's a wonderful thing to walk through the door and smell the aroma of juicy chicken simmering in tomato, onions, and spices. This slow cooker chicken recipe is simple and requires no prep work beyond twisting the lid off a jar of salsa. Serve with corn tortillas and your choice of fixings.

4 boneless, skinless chicken breasts
1 (16-oz) jar Chunky Salsa or your favorite salsa

**Optional Fixings:**
Corn or flour tortillas
Guacamole
Sour cream
Shredded Mexican Blend Cheese
Chopped fresh cilantro

1 Add chicken and salsa to your slow cooker.

2 Cook for 3 hours on high or 6-8 hours on low. If you're headed to work, leave it on low and it will be cooked by the time you come home (cooking a little longer is OK).

3 Serve with tortillas and other fixings as desired.

Prep time: 2 minutes
Hands-off cooking time: 6-8 hours
Serves 8

Nutrition Snapshot
Per serving: 81 calories, 2 g fat, 0 g saturated fat,
13 g protein, 2 g carbs, 0 g fiber, 4 g sugar,
460 mg sodium

Serve with
corn tortillas

Chipotle Shrimp and Grits

Our version of classic "shrimp and grits" is spiced up shrimp served over slices of polenta. Trader Joe's polenta is available in ready-to-use tubes that we cook up hot and crispy, seasoned with a dash of Taco Seasoning. Shrimp is cooked until just tender and drizzled with a creamy sauce made of sour cream and smoky chipotle salsa.

1 (1-lb) bag uncooked (large to colossal) shrimp, tail on or off, thawed
1 cup Chipotle Salsa or your favorite salsa
¼ cup sour cream
1 (18-oz) tube pre-cooked polenta
¼ + ½ tsp Taco Seasoning Mix, divided
1 ½ Tbsp olive oil, divided

1 Heat salsa in small saucepan. Stir in sour cream, remove from heat, and set aside.

2 Cut polenta into 12 rounds. Sprinkle lightly with ¼ tsp Taco Seasoning.

3 Heat 1 Tbsp oil in large skillet over high heat and pan fry polenta rounds until golden (3 min each side). Transfer to plate and set aside.

4 Pat dry shrimp with paper towels. Season shrimp with remaining ½ tsp Taco Seasoning. Add remaining oil to same skillet over high heat, add shrimp, and cook for 3 minutes or until cooked and opaque. Do not overcook shrimp.

5 Place shrimp over polenta rounds, drizzle with salsa mixture, and serve immediately.

Prep and cooking time: 20 minutes
Serves 4

Nutrition Snapshot
Per serving: 226 calories, 8 g fat, 2 g saturated fat, 19 g protein, 17 g carbs, 2 g fiber, 5 g sugar, 515 mg sodium

Gluten Free

Chicken with Browned Onions

This basic chicken recipe is a versatile main dish that pairs well with anything from risotto to potatoes to pasta to veggies. The onions cook and brown alongside the chicken, resulting in deeply flavored, dark onions that are sweet but also tangy from the lemon juice added to the pan.

1 lb boneless, skinless chicken thighs (4-6 thighs)
1 tsp salt
½ tsp black pepper
1 Tbsp olive oil
1 medium onion, sliced
Juice of 1 large lemon (about 3 Tbsp lemon juice)
1 clove garlic or 1 cube Frozen Crushed Garlic

1 Season chicken with salt and pepper.

2 Heat oil in large skillet over high heat. Add onion and chicken to pan. Cook 3 minutes without moving, then flip chicken (it should start to have a nice color on the seared side). Cook 3 minutes more.

3 Add lemon juice and garlic, moving chicken around and loosening onions from the pan. Flip chicken one last time, lowering heat to medium. Cook 3 minutes more or until chicken is done.

Prep and cooking time: 15 minutes
Serves 4

Nutrition Snapshot
Per serving: 114 calories, 5 g fat, 1 g saturated fat, 14 g protein, 3 g carbs, 0 g fiber, 1 g sugar, 445 mg sodium

Grilled Mac-n-Cheese Sandwich

What happens when mac-n-cheese meets a grilled cheese sandwich? Comfort-food heaven! Mac-n-cheese and bacon slices are placed in between slices of sourdough bread and grilled to golden, buttery perfection. This sandwich is perfect for leftover mac-n-cheese (recipe for an easy homemade version on page 145), and easy to make individually or for a group. For the ultimate comfort food combination, pair with a bowl of tomato soup.

For each sandwich:

2 slices sourdough bread

1 Tbsp butter

½ cup prepared mac-n-cheese

⅓ cup Shredded 3 Cheese Blend

2 slices Fully Cooked Bacon, crisped in microwave or pan

To make 6 sandwiches: Use 1 box mac-n-cheese (prepared with milk and butter), 1 sourdough boule, 2 cups shredded cheese, and 1 package bacon.

1 Prepare mac-n-cheese according to package instructions, or reheat leftover mac-n-cheese.

2 Melt butter in pan or cast iron skillet over medium heat. Place two slices of bread in pan and top both slices with shredded cheese. When cheese begins to melt, cover one slice with mac-n-cheese and bacon; top with other bread slice. Grill on both sides until golden.

Nutrition Snapshot

Per serving: 384 calories, 17 g fat,
9 g saturated fat, 17 g protein, 24 g carbs,
1 g fiber, 1 g sugar, 639 mg sodium

Omit bacon or substitute vegetarian bacon

Use gluten-free bread and gluten-free mac-n-cheese

Steak Salad

Steak salad is a great way to enjoy rich steaks, served over vibrant greens and meaty tomatoes. Peppery arugula and ripe heirloom tomatoes add a tasty and fresh balance to a flavorful steak. Choose steaks that aren't too thick so you can cook them in a pan without finishing them in the oven. This recipe is also a fantastic way to use up leftover steak for lunch the next day—no need to reheat the steak; just slice thinly and add to your salad.

2 (½-lb each) steaks, not too thick (1 inch or less)

1 tsp salt

1 tsp freshly ground black pepper

1 Tbsp olive oil

1 (7-oz) bag Arugula leaves or other greens (about 5 cups)

4 Heirloom tomatoes or regular tomatoes, sliced

⅓ cup Balsamic Vinaigrette dressing (or make your own page 66)

¼ cup Crumbed Gorgonzola cheese (or crumbled goat cheese if you prefer a milder cheese)

1 Pat steaks dry. Season with salt and pepper.

2 Heat oil in a heavy pan such as a cast iron skillet over high heat. When oil is very hot, add steaks. Sear for 3 minutes, flip steak, and sear for an additional 2 minutes. For 1-inch steaks, they should be medium-rare at this point and feel soft but springy to the touch. For medium-well, add an extra 30 seconds to each side.

3 Remove steaks from heat, drape with foil, and let rest for at least 5 minutes.

4 Meanwhile, toss arugula with dressing and divide between 4 plates. Add tomatoes.

5 Cut steak into thin slices and arrange over greens. Top each salad with 1 Tbsp cheese. Drizzle with extra dressing and sprinkle with extra freshly ground pepper if desired.

Prep and cooking time: 15 minutes
Serves 4

Nutrition Snapshot

Per serving: 299 calories, 14 g fat, 3 g saturated fat,
35 g protein, 7 g carbs, 1 g fiber, 6 g sugar, 702 mg sodium

 Some Gorgonzola cheeses are not gluten free.

Sausage Mushroom Calzone

A calzone is essentially a folded pizza, traditionally stuffed with ingredients you would find on a pizza: cheese, meats, and veggies. This delicious variation is filled with sausage, mozzarella, mushrooms, and tangy sauce. Trader Joe's Sweet Italian Sausage has bits of green and red pepper, adding taste without adding work. Ready-to-use pizza dough makes it quick and easy to assemble. Top calzones with warm marinara, or put marinara in a bowl for dipping and pouring.

1 (1-lb) bag refrigerated Ready to Bake Pizza Dough

1 Tbsp olive oil

3 Sweet Italian Style chicken sausages, sliced

2 cups sliced crimini mushrooms

⅓ cup jarred marinara sauce, plus extra for dipping

1 cup shredded mozzarella cheese

1 Preheat oven to 450° F.

2 Heat oil in a skillet over medium-high heat. Add sausage and mushrooms; cook and stir for about 5 minutes until sausage is browned and mushrooms have cooked down. Stir in marinara sauce and remove from heat.

3 Divide dough in half, and roll out two 8–inch circles on a floured surface.

4 Divide sausage mixture between the two circles of dough. Sprinkle each with half the cheese. Fold dough over into classic crescent shape and crimp edges closed with fingers or a fork. Repeat for second calzone.

5 Bake calzones on lightly oiled baking sheet or pizza stone for 20 minutes or until top is golden.

Prep time: 10 minutes
Hands-off cooking time: 20 minutes
Makes 2 large calzones (Serves 4)

Nutrition Snapshot

Per serving: 346 calories, 11 g fat, 5 g saturated fat,
20 g protein, 39 g carbs, 2 g fiber, 2 g sugar, 626 mg sodium

Use Italian Sausage-less Sausage, or substitute additional veggies, spinach, or ricotta for sausage

Korean Carne

What happens when you use Korean bool kogi to make carne asada tacos?
Korean carne – a perfect marriage of cultures! Bool kogi is thinly sliced marinated boneless beef ribs that are often grilled, chopped, and used in Asian-style lettuce wraps. We broke the rules and paired bool kogi with corn tortillas, pico de gallo, and creamy avocados. Thanks to Sean Coveney of Leucadia, CA, for coining the title and inspiring this delicious fusion dish.

1 (1.5-lb) pkg refrigerated Bool Kogi (Korean marinated boneless beef ribs)

8 small corn tortillas

4 cups shredded Romaine or iceberg lettuce

2 ripe avocados, diced

1 (12-oz) container refrigerated Pico de Gallo

1 Cook meat in heavy pan over high heat or use grill. Remove from heat and let rest for 2 minutes.

2 Meanwhile, heat corn tortillas (see note below).

3 Cut meat into strips or dice. Divide meat among tortillas. Top with lettuce, avocado, and 2-3 Tbsp pico de gallo. Serve immediately.

Prep and cooking time: 10 minutes
Makes 8 tacos

Nutrition Snapshot
Per serving: 394 calories, 24 g fat, 7 g saturated fat,
18 g protein, 31 g carbs, 7 g fiber, 7 g sugar, 758 mg sodium

Helpful Tip: Corn tortillas are stiff and rubbery until they are heated. An easy way to heat a large number of corn tortillas is to steam them in the microwave. First, separate tortillas from each other. Drizzle 2-3 Tbsp water on a clean kitchen towel. Fan out the tortillas slightly, wrap the towel around them, and heat in microwave for 1½-2 minutes. Steamed tortillas will stay warm for 10 minutes.

G
Gluten Free

Substitute another meat,
as Bool Kogi marinade
contains soy sauce

Speedy Weeknight Chili

Who says chili takes all day to make? Thick, hearty chili can be ready in about 25 minutes from start to finish! We start with a base of Mirepoix (chopped onion, carrots, and celery, available in one convenient container at Trader Joe's), and we add ground beef, beans, and salsa. The final ingredient is a can of refried beans, a great shortcut to getting that thick chili texture in minutes flat.

1 (1-lb) pkg ground beef (we used 85% lean) or ground turkey

1 Tbsp olive oil

1 (14.5-oz) container Mirepoix (or use 1 cup each chopped onion, celery, and carrot)

1 (15-oz) can black beans, rinsed and drained

½ cup Chunky Salsa or your favorite salsa

1 (16-oz) can Refried Black Beans with Jalapeno

1 Heat oil in saucepan or pot over high heat. Add mirepoix; cook and stir for about 5 minutes or until veggies are softened. Add beef; cook and stir, breaking up the beef until it is cooked thoroughly. Stir in black beans and salsa.

2 Add refried beans and ½ cup water; stir until well combined. If chili is too thick, add water a small amount at a time until you reach a desired consistency. Simmer covered over low heat for 10-15 minutes.

Prep time: 5 minutes
Cooking time: 20-25 minutes
Makes 6 cups of chili

Nutrition Snapshot

Per serving: 347 calories, 14 g fat, 5 g saturated fat,
24 g protein, 32 g carbs, 5 g fiber, 4 g sugar, 589 mg sodium

Gluten Free

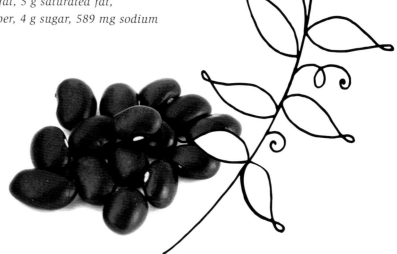

Cowboy Cornbread

This layered meal feels like the rustic American version of shepherd's pie. Imagine a rugged cowboy singing a sad song by a warm campfire. Well, this is what he's eating! Hearty chili is topped by a layer of sweet golden cornbread. Make your own chili (page 94) or call it a day and use canned chili.

6 cups of chili (either homemade or use three 15-oz cans of your favorite chili)

1 (15-oz) box cornbread mix (plus milk, eggs, and water per instructions)

1 Preheat oven to 350° F.

2 Heat chili in saucepan and spread in the bottom of an 8x10-inch baking dish.

3 Prepare cornbread batter according to package instructions. Spread batter evenly and smoothly over chili.

4 Bake for 35 minutes until cornbread is golden and toothpick inserted in cornbread comes out clean.

Prep time: 5 minutes
Cooking time: 35 minutes
Serves 8

Nutrition Snapshot

Nutritional information varies based on chili.
Using our recipe for Speedy Weeknight Chili,
Per serving: 553 calories, 25 g fat, 5 g saturated fat,
22 g protein, 68 g carbs, 5 g fiber, 20 g sugar, 723 mg sodium

Use vegetarian
chili

Mahi Mahi with Creamy Leeks

Mahi Mahi is seasoned simply and cooked in a butter-oil combination, served over a delicious bed of creamy leeks. They key to this simple yet elegant recipe is to cook the leeks nearly all the way beforehand to develop their rich flavor and prevent the cooked fish from sitting around getting cold. White wine and cream add depth that nicely complements the fish.

4 fillets Mahi-Mahi (about 1 lb, thawed if frozen)

½ tsp salt

½ tsp black pepper

2 Tbsp olive oil, divided

1 Tbsp butter

2 trimmed leeks, chopped (about 3 cups)

⅓ cup white wine

⅓ cup heavy cream

2 Tbsp chopped fresh chives as garnish (optional)

Lemon slices for garnish (optional)

1   Pat dry and season fish with salt and pepper. Set aside.

2   Heat 1 Tbsp oil in a pan over medium-high heat. Add leeks; cook and stir for 8 minutes, adding 1-2 Tbsp of water as you cook to speed softening of leeks. Move leeks to a plate and set aside.

3   In the same pan, add 1 Tbsp oil and 1 Tbsp butter over medium heat. When hot, add fish. Cook 2 minutes on one side, flip, and cook an additional 1-2 minutes until fish is opaque and flakes easily (time depends on thickness of fillets). Place fillets on plate and tent with foil to keep warm.

4   Return leeks to pan. Add wine; cook and stir for 3 minutes more or until wine evaporates. Stir in cream and cook a minute longer until heated through. Divide leeks between four plates and top with fish. Garnish with chives and lemon slices.

Prep time: 5 minutes
Cooking time: 15 minutes
Serves 4

Nutrition Snapshot
Per serving: 162 calories, 14 g fat, 5 g saturated fat,
1 g protein, 7 g carbs, 1 g fiber, 2 g sugar, 413 mg sodium

Gluten Free

Apricot Glazed Pork Chops

Pork chops are a quick, easy, and relatively inexpensive weeknight meal. Center cut (boneless) pork loins in our apricot glaze might even pass for a fancy weekend meal. Pork and fruit sauces are a classic pairing. Our glaze is made with apricot preserves balanced with the tangy kick of Dijon, apple cider vinegar, and black pepper. You'll want to serve this dish over potatoes or rice so you can soak up every bit of the tasty sauce.

1.3 lbs thick cut boneless pork loin chops (3 chops) or pork cutlets (5-6 cutlets)
½ tsp salt
½ tsp black pepper
1 Tbsp olive oil
⅓ cup apricot preserves
⅓ cup chicken broth
1 Tbsp apple cider vinegar
1 Tbsp Dijon mustard (we like coarse-ground "country Dijon")

1 In a bowl, whisk together apricot preserves, broth, vinegar, and mustard. Set aside.

2 Season pork with salt and pepper. Heat oil in pan over high heat. Add pork to pan and cook 3 minutes without moving. Flip and cook 2 minutes without moving. Lower heat to medium and cook 2 minutes more, checking pork for doneness (no longer pink with an internal temperature of 145° F). Do not overcook pork as it will become very tough. If using cutlets, cook 2 minutes each side over high heat.

3 Remove chops from pan and set on plate. Turn heat to low. Add apricot mixture to pan; stir until mixture reduces by half (about 2 minutes) and has thickened. Return chops to pan, coating with glaze.

Prep time: 5 minutes
Cooking time: 10 minutes
Serves 3

Nutrition Snapshot
Per serving: 290 calories, 12 g fat, 3 g saturated fat,
34 g protein, 13 g carbs, 0 g fiber, 12 g sugar, 770 mg sodium

Gluten Free

Use gluten-free
chicken broth

Spicy Sesame Noodles

Got a craving for Chinese takeout? Satisfy it with these take-out style noodles that are prepared simply with Soyaki teriyaki sauce, sesame oil, red pepper flakes, and crunchy green onion. The noodles pair perfectly with chicken or salmon, or any Asian main course. They're so good that people will be knocking on *your* door for takeout.

1 (16-oz) pkg spaghetti

¼ cup Soyaki teriyaki sauce

2 Tbsp toasted sesame oil

½–1 tsp red pepper flakes

4 green onions, chopped (about   cup)

1 Prepare pasta according to package instructions; drain and place in serving bowl.

2 Combine Soyaki, sesame oil, and red pepper flakes; pour over pasta and toss to coat. Stir in green onion. Serve warm or cold.

Prep time: 5 minutes
Hands-off cooking time: 8-10 minutes
Serves 6

Nutrition Snapshot

Per serving: 348 calories, 7 g fat, 1 g saturated fat, 12 g protein, 60 g carbs, 3 g fiber, 6 g sugar, 347 mg sodium

Use gluten-free pasta. Gluten-free teriyaki sauce is available at other grocers

Brown Sugar Salmon

Sweet salmon in a snap? That's easy! Sassy Dijon mustard and brown sugar create a tangy sweet sauce that will make you want to lick your plate. Marinating is not necessary, so you can literally have dinner on the table in minutes. Try it with our Springtime Spinach Rice (page 184) or Middle Eastern Dill Rice (page 176).

4 (6-oz) salmon fillets
Generous pinch of salt
Pinch of black pepper
2 Tbsp brown sugar
2 Tbsp Dijon mustard
2 tsp grated ginger or 1 tsp powdered ginger (use less for milder flavor)

1 Preheat oven to 400° F. Line a baking sheet with foil for easy cleanup.

2 Season salmon with salt and pepper; place on baking sheet. Whisk together sugar, mustard, and ginger. Spread evenly on salmon fillets.

3 Bake for 10 minutes. Salmon will continue to cook after it's removed from heat, so it's okay if the center is a bit translucent. Do not overcook.

Prep time: 5 minutes
Hands-off cooking time: 7-9 minutes
Serves 4

Nutrition Snapshot
Per serving: 374 calories, 22 g fat, 5 g saturated fat,
34 g protein, 5 g carbs, 0 g fiber, 4 g sugar, 193 mg sodium

Sticky Chicky

The kids love asking for "Sticky Chicky," our version of Asian take-out honey sesame chicken. Serve over sticky rice or jasmine rice. Add an easy green by stir frying baby bok choy in the same pan immediately after finishing the chicken.

1 lb skinless, boneless chicken (about 2 breasts or 4 thighs)
3 Tbsp Soyaki teriyaki sauce
2 Tbsp honey
1 Tbsp ketchup
3 Tbsp flour
2 Tbsp olive oil
¼ cup chopped green onions (optional)

1 Add Soyaki, honey, and ketchup to a bowl, whisk until smooth.

2 Cut chicken into bite size pieces. Coat in flour.

3 Heat oil in non-stick skillet over high heat. Add chicken and brown on both sides (about 3 minutes each side). Lower heat to medium and cook an extra 4 minutes until pieces are cooked through.

4 Turn heat off. Drizzle Soyaki mixture over chicken, gently stirring for about 1 minute until sauce is thick and clinging to the chicken. (Residual heat of pan should be enough to thicken the sauce.) Garnish with green onions.

Prep and cooking time: 10-15 minutes
Serves 4

Nutrition Snapshot
Per serving: 245 calories, 9 g fat, 1 g saturated fat, 15 g protein, 22 g carbs, 0 g fiber, 20 g sugar, 465 mg sodium

Country Potato Quiche

Quiche is an appealing, versatile dish that is suitable for brunch, lunch, and even dinner. This recipe can serve as your simple 5-ingredient foundation recipe. Just swap out potatoes and green beans for any other combination of mixed vegetables and voila, you are a genius with a completely different quiche. Serve with a simple salad to round out the meal.

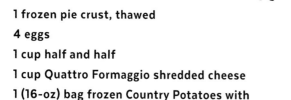

1 frozen pie crust, thawed

4 eggs

1 cup half and half

1 cup Quattro Formaggio shredded cheese

1 (16-oz) bag frozen Country Potatoes with
    Haricots Verts & Wild Mushrooms, thawed

1 Preheat oven to 375° F.

2 Press pie crust into a 9-inch pie dish.

3 Whisk together eggs and half and half. Stir in cheese and potato mix. Pour mixture into pie crust, making sure potato pieces are distributed evenly.

4 Bake for 40 minutes or until a knife inserted in center comes out clean.

5 Let cool for a few minutes, then slice and serve.

Substitutions: Use any other 16-oz frozen potato mix such as Garlic Potatoes. If using an unseasoned vegetable mix in place of the Country Potatoes mix, add ½ tsp each salt and pepper.

Prep time: 5-10 minutes
Hands-off cooking time: 40 minutes
Serves 8

Nutrition Snapshot
Per serving: 392 calories, 28 g fat, 15 g saturated fat,
12 g protein, 25 g carbs, 3 g fiber, 3 g sugar, 280 mg sodium

Vegetarian   Gluten Free

    Use gluten-free pie crust
    available at other grocers

Linguine with Bruschetta and Pine Nuts

Cooks seeking an easy meal have long turned to pasta topped with canned tomato sauce. Our twist is to use fresh bruschetta sauce enlivened by pine nuts and fresh basil. It's a simple change that makes this pasta feel more special and gourmet.

Enjoy as is, or use as a base to add grilled eggplant, cooked chicken, sliced sausage, or scallops.

1 (1-lb) package linguine or other pasta
1 (14.5-oz) container refrigerated Fresh Bruschetta Sauce
½ cup toasted pine nuts
½ cup chopped fresh basil
½ cup shredded Parmesan cheese

1 Prepare pasta according to packaging instructions; drain and place in serving bowl.

2 Add bruschetta sauce to the pasta and toss well. Sprinkle with pine nuts, basil, and Parmesan. Toss again.

Prep time: 5 minutes
Hands-off cooking time: 8-10 minutes
Serves 6

Nutrition Snapshot

Per serving: 498 calories, 22 g fat, 3 g saturated fat, 15 g protein, 60 g carbs, 3 g fiber, 5 g sugar, 469 mg sodium

Use gluten-free pasta

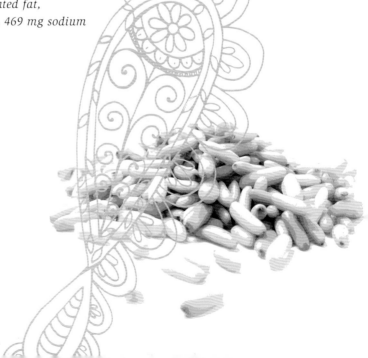

Foolproof Cooked Plain Chicken

Once a week, usually when Deana is waiting for something to finish on the stove or in the oven, she cooks up a quick batch of chicken thighs on the stove and dices them. It takes about 12 minutes and she has plain diced chicken to use all week in wraps, in salads, or in other recipes. Compared to chicken breasts, thighs pack in more flavor at less cost. They stay juicy and are pretty forgiving if slightly overcooked. If you still prefer breasts, you can cook them with this same method. Just increase cooking time in final step by 5 minutes or more depending on thickness of breasts.

5-6 boneless skinless chicken thighs (about 1.5-2 lbs)

1 Tbsp olive oil, divided

1 tsp salt

½ tsp black pepper

1 Drizzle ½ Tbsp oil on chicken and sprinkle with salt and pepper. Rub chicken to distribute oil and seasonings evenly.

2 Choose a large skillet that has a lid. Heat skillet over high heat. Add remaining ½ Tbsp oil and add chicken; cook for 2 minutes.

3 Flip chicken, cover pan with lid, and lower heat to low. Cook for an additional 10 minutes over low heat without lifting the lid or peeking underneath. After the 10 minutes are up, check chicken for doneness.

Note: 6 chicken thighs will yield about 4 cups of diced chicken.

Prep time: 5 minutes
Hands-off cooking time: 12 minutes
Serves 6

Nutrition Snapshot

Per serving: 102 calories, 5 g fat, 1 g saturated fat,
14 g protein, 0 g carbs, 0 g fiber, 0 g sugar, 439 mg sodium

Gluten Free

Green Chile Chicken Enchiladas

Enchiladas are a surprisingly easy way to make a tasty, hearty meal. Chicken and a delicious sauce are rolled up inside flour tortillas, then topped with cheese and more salsa. Mix it up with different green salsas from Trader Joe's: mild Salsa Verde or the spicier Hatch Valley Salsa made with green chiles from the famous Hatch Valley region of New Mexico.

1 (16-oz) container Just Chicken, or 4 cups diced cooked/leftover chicken (page 113)
6 medium (8-inch) flour tortillas
⅔ cup (4 oz) light or regular whipped cream cheese
1 (12-oz) jar Hatch Valley Salsa (spicy) or Salsa Verde (mild), divided
1 cup shredded pepper jack cheese

1   Preheat oven to 350° F.

2   Dice or shred chicken into small pieces. In a bowl, combine chicken, cream cheese, and ½ cup of salsa. Stir until well combined.

3   Spread 2-3 Tbsp salsa on bottom of 8x10-inch baking dish. Fill each tortilla with about ⅔ cup of chicken filling; roll tortilla tightly and place in pan seam side down. Repeat for remaining tortillas, placing side by side in pan.

4   Pour remaining salsa (about 1 cup) over rolled tortillas and sprinkle with cheese.

5   Wrap tightly with foil and bake for 30 minutes. Remove foil and bake for additional 10 minutes until cheese is melted and bubbly at edges.

Prep time: 10 min
Hands-off cooking time: 40 minutes
Serves 6

Nutrition Snapshot
Per serving: 365 calories, 14 g fat, 5 g saturated fat,
25 g protein, 31 g carbs, 1 g fiber, 4 g sugar, 771 mg sodium

Turkey Roll Ups

Every year, we head to the Los Angeles Times Festival of Books, one of the biggest book festivals in the country. We are always so busy at our booth that we never have time to leave for lunch. So we've gotten in the habit of packing our own, and for the last 7 years, this simple roll-up has been our go-to lunch. Cucumber adds just enough crunch and moisture to balance the turkey and tortilla, and creamy Havarti cheese takes away the need for any condiments like mayo. Maybe it's because we're starving at the end of the day, but every year Wona takes a bite and declares, "OMG, this is the best combo ever. We have to put this in our next book." And here it is!

For each sandwich:

1 flour tortilla

1 slice Havarti cheese

2 slices roasted turkey breast (deli sliced)

1 Persian cucumber, sliced down the length

1 Place tortilla on plate or counter. Cut cheese in half and place along center of tortilla. Top with turkey slices and cucumber.

2 Roll tortilla tightly and slice in half.

Prep time: 5 minutes
Serves 1

Nutrition Snapshot

Per serving: 366 calories, 14 g fat, 6 g saturated fat, 28 g protein, 29 g carbs, 3 g fiber, 1 g sugar, 567 mg sodium

Portabella Quesadilla

Portabellas are large, hearty mushrooms that are delicious and almost meaty in texture, making them popular in sandwiches or as a substitute for a burger. We combined them with fire-roasted peppers and onions to fill a quesadilla. Slightly spicy pepper jack cheese adds even more flavor to this crispy folded tortilla.

2 large flour tortillas

1 Tbsp olive oil

1 large portabella mushroom cap with stem removed, sliced

2 cups frozen Fire Roasted Peppers and Onions

1 Tbsp soy sauce

½ cup shredded pepper jack cheese

1 Heat oil in skillet over medium-high to high heat. Add mushroom and frozen peppers and onions. Drizzle with soy sauce. Stir until mushrooms are cooked, veggies are hot, and extra liquid has evaporated (about 5 minutes). Remove mixture from pan and set aside.

2 Wipe skillet clean and place tortilla inside. Sprinkle one half of tortilla with ¼ cup of cheese and spread half the mushroom mixture on top. When cheese is melted, fold tortilla in half and flip to toast both sides. Repeat with second tortilla.

Prep and cooking time: 15 minutes
Makes 2 quesadillas

Nutrition Snapshot
Per serving: 391 calories, 20 g fat, 7 g saturated fat,
16 g protein, 43 g carbs, 6 g fiber, 7 g sugar, 905 mg sodium

  Use brown rice tortillas and substitute tamari for soy sauce

Chicken Cordon Bleu Panini

Originally from Italy, a panini is a pressed and toasted sandwich that is golden, crispy, and warm. They are usually made with a panini press, but a stovetop version yields the same result and is equally delicious. This panini is filled with our version of the iconic Chicken Cordon Bleu (breaded chicken stuffed with ham and Swiss cheese). Zingy mustard offsets the rich filling.

1-2 pieces Frozen Breaded Chicken Tenderloin, or leftover breaded chicken

1 par-baked Panini Rustic Rolls (or any bread – even sandwich slices)

2 tsp Sweet and Hot Mustard or mayo

1 slice ham

1 slice Swiss cheese

1 Heat chicken according to package instructions.

2 Cut panini roll open. Spread mustard on bottom half. Layer ham, cheese, and 1-2 pieces chicken depending on size. Assemble number of desired sandwiches.

3 If not using a panini press, use a cast-iron pan. Lightly spray or oil the pan and place over medium heat. Place sandwich(es) in pan and press with a second cast-iron pan placed on top (or use something heavy like a pie pan weighed down with canned goods) and toast for 2-3 minutes until golden and crisp. Flip and toast the other side.

Prep and cooking time: 10 minutes
Makes 1 sandwich

Nutrition Snapshot

Per serving: 445 calories, 14 g fat, 6 g saturated fat, 38 g protein, 48 g carbs, 4 g fiber, 0 g sugar, 1030 mg sodium

Use gluten-free
sandwich bread and
grilled (unbreaded)
chicken

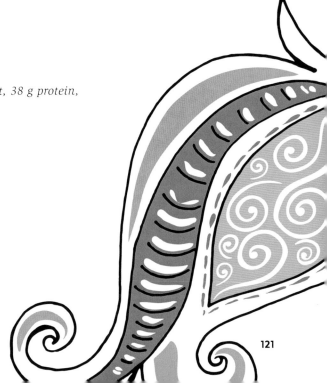

Granny Smith Apple Chicken Pitas

Wona first had these sandwiches while backpacking through the Sierras with her friend Gloria Lee of Oakland, CA. Gloria is the ultimate gourmand, even when camping! The secret is not in the depth of your hunger (pretty deep on the trail), but in the crunchy tart Granny Smith apples, which impart flavor in every bite. For camping trips or hikes, you can prepare this sandwich using canned chicken. Gloria often makes a creamier version using a generous dollop of yogurt and a sprinkle of curry powder.

2 cups diced cooked chicken
1 large Granny Smith apple, diced
Juice of 1 lemon (2 Tbsp lemon juice)
½ tsp salt
½ tsp 21 Seasoning Salute or other seasoning
4 pita pockets, whole wheat or white

1 Mix chicken, apple, and lemon juice. Season with salt and seasoning.

2 Spoon chicken mixture into pita pockets. Serve immediately.

Prep time: 5 minutes
Serves 4

Nutrition Snapshot

Per serving: 349 calories, 8 g fat, 2 g saturated fat, 29 g protein, 40 g carbs, 6 g fiber, 7 g sugar, 594 mg sodium

 Use gluten-free bread or serve on lettuce leaves

Lightened Up Italian Sausage and Peppers Pasta

Jennifer Drummond, health food blogger (PeanutButterAndPeppers.com), created this satisfying meal using TJ's spicy chicken sausage which is only 140 calories a link, compared to 300 + calories in normal Italian sausages. She also lightened this dish using quinoa pasta. It has all the flavors of an Italian sausage sub but is easier on your waistline.

4 oz quinoa pasta or spaghetti

1 ½ Tbsp olive oil, divided

2 Spicy Italian Chicken Sausages, cut into slices

1 green bell pepper, cut into bite-size chunks

½ onion, sliced thin

1 Tbsp chopped fresh basil

1-2 Tbsp shaved Parmesan cheese (optional)

1 In a large pot, bring about 6 cups of water to a boil. Add pasta and cook until tender, about 10 minutes. Drain pasta.

2 Meanwhile, in a large skillet over medium heat, add ½ Tbsp oil and warm for 30 seconds, add sausage, bell pepper, and onion. Cook until vegetables are tender and sausage is cooked, about 10 minutes.

3 Add cooked pasta and 1 Tbsp oil to skillet with vegetables and sausage. Mix together until well combined.

4 Serve immediately. Top with basil and Parmesan.

Prep and cooking time: 25 minutes
Serves 2

Nutrition Snapshot
Per serving: 453 calories, 20 g fat, 4 g saturated fat, 23 g protein, 6 g carbs, 3 g fiber, 3 g sugar, 593 mg sodium

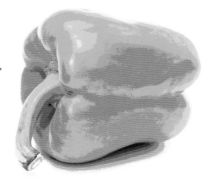

Use Italian Sausage-
less Sausage

Shrimp Scampi

Shrimp Scampi is elegant enough for company. It looks like you fussed, when in reality it's easy enough to prepare for a midweek meal. When Argentinian rock shrimp is available, try using it in this recipe for a lobster-flavored version.

1 lb raw shrimp, thawed if frozen

3 garlic cloves, crushed, or 3 cubes frozen Crushed Garlic

¼ tsp black pepper

2 Tbsp olive oil

2 Tbsp butter

½ cup white wine

¼ cup grated Parmesan cheese

2 Tbsp chopped fresh parsley

1 Toss shrimp, garlic, and pepper. Set aside.

2 Heat oil and butter in a large sauté pan over high heat. Add shrimp and cook for 2 minutes, stirring constantly.

3 Add wine. Cook for another 1-2 minutes until shrimp is opaque.

4 Sprinkle with Parmesan and parsley. Serve over rice or pasta.

Prep time: 5 minutes
Cooking time: 5 minutes
Serves 4

Variation: Substitute ¼ cup freshly squeezed lemon juice for the wine.

Nutrition Snapshot
Per serving: 248 calories, 13 g fat, 6 g saturated fat,
25 g protein, 1 g carbs, 0 g fiber, 0 g sugar, 237 mg sodium

G
Gluten Free

Tortilla Española (Spanish Omelette)

Wona's friend Esther San Miguel is a terrific cook from Barcelona, Spain. She is famous in her social circles for making her home country's signature dish, delicious tortilla Española. In Mexican cooking, the tortilla is the thin flat bread we know, but in Spanish cooking, a tortilla is a thick omelet cut into wedges. Esther makes her tortilla without onion, but we love the classic combo of fried potato and onion. Serve with a green salad and crusty bread. Cha cha cha!

4 large red potatoes
1 large onion (optional)
6 large eggs
⅔ cup olive oil or vegetable oil
½ tsp salt
½ tsp black pepper

1 Peel potatoes and slice thinly. Slice onions thinly. Speed up the process by using a mandoline or the side of a box grater.

2 Choose an 8- to 9-inch saucepan or skillet with a cover. Pour in oil and heat over medium high heat. Test the oil by dropping in a piece of potato: when the oil sizzles around it, you've reached the right heat. Add potatoes and onion, lowering heat to medium-low.

3 Cook potatoes and onion, stirring frequently, until potatoes are cooked and begin to brown, about 20-30 minutes. When potatoes are soft and lightly browned, drain vegetables in a large colander set over a bowl. Reserve drained oil.

4 Crack eggs into a mixing bowl and whisk with salt and pepper. Add cooked potatoes and onions; mix to combine.

5 Return skillet to medium flame and add 1Tbsp reserved oil. When pan is hot, pour in egg mixture. Reduce heat to low, cover, and cook eggs 10 minutes until bottom is almost set. Run spatula along sides and under omelet to make sure it isn't sticking to the pan.

6 To flip, place a plate over the pan. Holding the pan tightly to the plate (use oven mitts), flip omelet onto plate (raw side on plate). Slide omelet back into skillet, raw side down, using a spatula to slide omelet off plate. Round edges with a spatula for a pretty tortilla. Cook 10 minutes longer until both sides are done.

Prep time: 15 minutes
Cooking time: 30-45 minutes
Serves 6

Nutrition Snapshot
Per serving: 305 calories, 11 g fat, 2 g saturated fat, 11 g protein, 1 g carbs, 3 g fiber, 3 g sugar, 288 mg sodium

 Vegetarian Gluten Free

Curried Kale and Sweet Potatoes

This dish is chock full of minerals and vitamins from the dark leafy kale and deep orange sweet potatoes. Its taste is as complex as its color thanks to curry and chutney, which add spice and a sweet kick that is irresistible. If you have leftovers, assemble burritos for lunch the next day. Simply combine vegetables with quinoa, rice, or lentils, and wrap the savory combo in a tortilla.

1 (10-oz) bag kale
3 sweet potatoes, peeled and cut in 1-inch chunks
1 (15-oz) jar Masala Simmer Sauce or Curry Simmer Sauce
Half (9-oz) jar Mango Ginger Chutney, about ½ cup
⅓ cup pepitas (pumpkin seeds), optional

1 Pour simmer sauce and 1 cup water into large saucepan.

2 Add kale, sweet potatoes, and chutney. Stir and bring to a boil.

3 Reduce heat to medium low, cover, and cook for 20 minutes until potatoes are cooked.

4 Sprinkle pepitas on top and serve.

Prep time: 10 minutes
Hands-off cooking time: 20 minutes
Serves 6

Variation: Try using butternut squash instead of sweet potatoes.

Nutrition Snapshot
Per serving: 160 calories, 3 g fat, 1 g saturated fat, 4 g protein, 8 g carbs, 4 g fiber, 15 g sugar, 359 mg sodium

Chili Dog Casserole

This casserole is an easy way to satisfy a chili cheese dog craving, with less mess. To cut down on the saltiness of canned chili, we mix in a can of diced tomatoes. If you're using your own homemade chili (such as Speedy Weeknight Chili page 94) use 3-4 cups and omit tomatoes.

8 hot dogs, any kind (turkey, beef, chicken, or vegetarian)
4 large flour tortillas, halved, or 8 corn tortillas
1 (15-oz) can chili (we like Trader Joe's vegetarian chili)
1 (14.5-oz) can diced tomatoes, no salt added
¾ cup shredded cheese, such as Fancy Shredded Mexican Blend

1 Preheat oven to 350° F.

2 Combine chili and tomatoes. Spread one cup chili mixture into a 9x13-inch baking dish.

3 Roll hot dogs in tortillas and arrange in baking pan.

4 Pour remaining chili mixture on top of wrapped hot dogs. Sprinkle cheese on top.

5 Cover with foil and bake for 30 minutes until warmed through. Remove foil during last 10 minutes for cheese to brown.

Prep time: 5 minutes
Hands-off cooking time: 30 minutes
Makes 8 chili dog rolls

Nutrition Snapshot
Per chili dog roll: 252 calories, 8 g fat, 2 g saturated fat, 19 g protein, 17 g carbs, 2 g fiber, 5 g sugar, 940 mg sodium

Use vegetarian hot dogs and vegetarian chili

Use corn tortillas, or omit tortillas

Pesto Baked Chicken

Pesto is an Italian sauce made of crushed basil, garlic, pine nuts, and Parmesan cheese. It's one of the most versatile sauces ever invented. We enjoy it mixed with pasta (try our Arugula and Peas Pasta Salad on page 152), stirred into soups, spread on sandwiches, or as a condiment to add scrumptious flavor to otherwise bland chicken. This dish looks (and tastes) quite fancy but takes only minutes to assemble and bake. Serve with pasta and asparagus.

2 skinless boneless chicken breasts
½ cup refrigerated Genova Pesto

1   Preheat oven to 400° F.

2   Using a meat pounder or a rolling pin, pound chicken breast to ½-inch thickness. Spread with pesto, reserving a spoonful to coat the tops. Roll up chicken and secure ends with toothpicks.

3   Spread reserved pesto on tops of chicken.

4   Bake for 20 minutes until chicken is done and juices run clear.

Prep time: 5-10 minutes
Hands-off cooking time: 20 minutes
Serves 4

Nutrition Snapshot

Per serving: 260 calories, 15 g fat, 2 g saturated fat,
29 g protein, 1 g carbs, 1 g fiber, 0 g sugar, 145 mg sodium

G Gluten Free

Italian Tuna Casserole

Tuna casserole doesn't have to be the mystery meal you remember from your childhood. For an updated version, we gave the school cafeteria standard an Italian twist. Savory tuna bits are evenly dispersed throughout the tomato-based sauce, and fresh bell pepper provides a fresh crunch in every bite. If you're not a fan of tuna, substitute crumbled Italian sausage.

1 (16-oz) bag pasta of any shape
1 (28-oz) jar marinara sauce
1 (5-oz) can tuna in oil, drained
1 bell pepper, any color
¼ cup grated or ½ cup shredded Parmesan cheese

1 Preheat oven to 350° F.

2 Cook pasta in salted water according to package directions. It makes a big difference in flavor if you salt the water, so don't skip this step.

3 While pasta is cooking, finely dice bell pepper. Combine marinara, tuna, and bell pepper in a large bowl.

4 Drain pasta, reserving a ladle of pasta water to thin out marinara mixture. Stir water into marinara mixture. Add pasta and stir to coat evenly. Pour mixture into 9x13-inch baking pan or casserole dish. Top with Parmesan.

5 Cover with foil and bake for 30 minutes until heated through.

Prep time: 10 minutes
Hands-off cooking time: 30 minutes
Serves 8

Nutrition Snapshot
Per serving: 286 calories, 6 g fat, 1 g saturated fat,
14 g protein, 49 g carbs, 2 g fiber, 3 g sugar, 430 mg sodium

Use gluten-
free pasta

Carnitas (Pulled Pork) Street Tacos

Mexican street tacos feature deliciously flavorful meats with simple toppings, usually cabbage and salsa. It's easy to recreate this cultural classic at home, thanks to Trader Joe's carnitas. These fall-apart moist and juicy pre-cooked portions of pork make an instant meal and are the perfect filling for our street tacos. We season cabbage with a light dressing of vinegar and salt. You can substitute refrigerated Cilantro Salad Dressing for a creamier touch.

1 (12-oz) pkg precooked Traditional Carnitas
12 corn tortillas
3 cups precut Shredded Cabbage
2 Tbsp apple cider vinegar or white vinegar
¼ tsp salt
1 (12-oz) container refrigerated Pico de Gallo

1 To prepare cabbage topping, toss cabbage with vinegar and salt. Set aside to let flavors meld.

2 Reheat carnitas in microwave or on stovetop. To reheat on stovetop, lightly grease a pan that has a cover and set over medium-high heat. Sear carnitas on both sides. Add ¼ cup water or broth and cover. Reduce heat to medium-low and heat until warmed through.

3 Using two forks, shred pork. It should fall apart easily.

4 Heat tortillas. See helpful tip on page 92.

5 To assemble each taco, stack two tortillas on a plate. Fill with carnitas, and top with cabbage and pico de gallo.

Note: Street tacos are generally served with 2 tortillas instead of one. We've heard all kinds of reasons, but our best guess is that it's to make the tortilla sturdier, as the juicy meats and salsas can make the inner tortilla fall apart. Whether you make them with 1 tortilla or 2, these street tacos are sure to be a hit!

Prep time: 5-10 minutes
Makes 6 tacos (with double tortillas)

Nutrition Snapshot

Per double-shelled taco: 240 calories, 9 g fat, 3 g saturated fat, 15 g protein, 25 g carbs, 3 g fiber, 3 g sugar, 334 mg sodium

Gluten Free

Salmon Salad

Meet our upscale version of tuna salad, using salmon. Salmon has a milder flavor than tuna and is a tasty twist on the ordinary classic. Whenever Wona puts salmon salad sandwiches in her kids' lunchboxes, it's one meal they don't trade. This recipe is a simple base from which to start, and you can add other vegetables such as celery, carrots, or bell peppers. If you like creamier salmon salad, add more mayonnaise.

2 fillets salmon, cooked, about 6 oz each
¼ cup finely chopped onion
¼ cup light or regular mayonnaise
⅓ cup pickled relish
Juice of ½ lemon (1 Tbsp lemon juice)
1 Tbsp olive oil
¼ tsp salt
1 Tbsp chopped fresh parsley or dill (optional)

1   Tear salmon into large flakes. Forks work well for this task.

2   Add salmon and remaining ingredients to a bowl. Mix well.

3   Serve on toasted bread or on bed of salad.

Tip: If you are starting with raw salmon, the easiest method is to poach. See poaching instructions on page 160.

Prep time: 10 minutes
Serves 4

Nutrition Snapshot

Per serving: 413 calories, 19 g fat,
3 g saturated fat, 20 g protein, 40 g carbs,
3 g fiber, 4 g sugar, 430 mg sodium

If serving on bread,
use gluten-free bread

Mexican Lasagna

Mexican meets Italian in this layered casserole, where tortillas take the place of lasagna noodles and Mexican-inspired flavors fill every layer. Wona learned to make this crowd-pleasing dish from her friend Gloria Lee, in Oakland, CA who can feed crowds without breaking a sweat. Gloria typically incorporates the season's freshest produce (see variations below), so don't be afraid to build on this basic recipe. Trader Joe's ready-to-use bottled Enchilada Sauce makes assembly a breeze. Make multiple batches for a large fiesta!

1 cooked chicken breast, shredded or cut into cubes (available pre-cooked refrigerated or frozen, or make your own page 113)
3 large flour tortillas, or 6 corn tortillas
1 (15-oz) can black beans, drained and rinsed
1 (12-oz) bottle Enchilada Sauce
1 cup shredded cheese, such as Fancy Shredded Mexican Blend

1 Preheat oven to 350° F.

2 Lightly grease a 9x13-inch baking pan or casserole dish. Make one layer of tortillas, cutting them in halves or quarters to fit the pan. Top with half the chicken, half the beans, half the Enchilada sauce, and half the cheese. Repeat to create top later, finishing with cheese.

3 Cover with foil and bake 30 minutes until cheese is bubbly. Remove foil during the last 10 minutes for cheese to brown.

Prep time: 20 minutes
Hands-off cooking time: 30 minutes
Serves 6

Variations: Add 1 cup cooked butternut squash, roasted bell peppers, or zucchini slices to the layers. Try using goat cheese instead of Mexican cheese.

Nutrition Snapshot

Per serving: 265 calories, 7 g fat, 2 g saturated fat, 22 g protein, 27 g carbs, 4 g fiber, 0 g sugar, 513 mg sodium

Vegetarian
Use chicken substitute or soy chorizo

G Gluten Free
Use corn tortillas and substitute your favorite salsa for Enchilada Sauce

Stovetop Mac and Cheese

Macaroni and cheese is a classic favorite among kids and adults alike. We love Alton Brown's recipe using eggs as the base for the creamy sauce and present a simplified version of his recipe below. The addition of Dijon mustard adds complex flavor, but you can leave it out if you predict that picky eaters will object. If the sauce is runny, let sit on the stove for a minute, so pasta has time to absorb sauce.

8 oz (half a 16-oz pkg) elbow macaroni, shells, or other shape pasta

2 eggs

½ tsp salt

¼ tsp black pepper

¾ cup milk

2 tsp Dijon mustard (optional)

¼ cup butter

2 cups shredded sharp cheddar cheese

1   Cook macaroni in salted water according to package directions. It makes a big difference in flavor if you salt the water, so don't skip this step.

2   While pasta is cooking, make cheese sauce base. Whisk eggs, salt, pepper, milk and mustard in a bowl.

3   Drain pasta and return to pot. Add butter and stir to coat. Stir in egg mixture and cheese. Cook over medium-low heat for 3 minutes, stirring frequently, until cheese is melted. Serve immediately.

Prep and cooking time: 20 minutes
Serves 4

Nutrition Snapshot

Per serving: 593 calories, 34 g fat, 19 g saturated fat,
26 g protein, 46 g carbs, 2 g fiber, 5 g sugar, 709 mg sodium

Vegetarian   Gluten Free

Use gluten-free
pasta

Lemon Sole

Sole is a flat white fish with a mild, buttery flavor. Tangy lemon, briny capers, and fresh parsley combine to make a delicious and brightly flavored sauce for this simple fish. Sole cooks very quickly, so it's the perfect weekday meal after a hectic workday. Serve with rice and lightly steamed green beans.

2 sole fillets, thawed if frozen

Pinch salt and pepper

2 Tbsp flour

2 Tbsp butter

Zest and juice of 1 large lemon

1 Tbsp capers, rinsed and drained (optional)

1 tsp chopped fresh parsley

1 Season fish with salt and pepper. Lightly coat with flour, shaking to remove excess flour.

2 Melt butter in large skillet over medium heat. Place sole in hot butter and cook for 2 minutes.

3 Flip fish. Add lemon zest, lemon juice, and capers. Continue cooking for 2-3 minutes until fish is done.

4 Sprinkle with parsley and serve.

Prep time: 5 minutes
Cooking time: 5 minutes
Serves 2

Nutrition Snapshot

Per serving: 288 calories, 14 g fat, 8 g saturated fat, 33 g protein, 8 g carbs, 1 g fiber, 1 g sugar, 211 mg sodium

Use gluten-free flour or almond meal

Eggplant Parmesan Lasagna

Lasagna doesn't get much easier than this! We use breaded eggplant cutlets as the pasta layer and smother them in ricotta, mozzarella, and marinara. You can leave out the spinach if you have spinach haters in the family. Assemble ahead of time and pop in the oven for an easy weeknight dinner.

2 (1-lb) cartons frozen Eggplant Cutlets, thawed (also OK if frozen, but add 15 minutes baking time)

1 (16-oz) container ricotta cheese

Half (16-oz) bag frozen Chopped Spinach, thawed and excess water squeezed out

1 (28-oz) jar marinara sauce

1 cup shredded mozzarella cheese

1 Preheat oven to 350°. Lightly grease a 9x13-inch baking pan or casserole dish.

2 Spoon some marinara sauce onto the bottom of baking pan, enough to cover lightly. Place 1 box of eggplant cutlets on the bottom, overlapping as needed. If cutlets are partially thawed, it will be easier to overlap.

3 Mix ricotta and spinach. Spread half this mixture on top of eggplant. Spread half the marinara sauce on top.

4 Repeat next layer. Sprinkle top with mozzarella.

5 Cover with foil and bake 45 minutes until cheese is bubbly. Remove foil for last 15 minutes for cheese to brown.

Prep time: 15 minutes
Hands-off baking time: 45 minutes
Serves 8

Nutrition Snapshot

Per serving: 385 calories, 21 g fat,
5 g saturated fat, 15 g protein, 34 g carbs,
5 g fiber, 8 g sugar, 973 mg sodium

Ham & Brie Sandwich

Wona's favorite sandwich throughout college was ham and Brie from the Au Bon Pain café in Harvard Square. The European combination of ham and Brie is wonderful cold or warm. Try it both ways because Brie cheese cold tastes entirely different than Brie cheese heated.

Per sandwich:

1 6-inch baguette portion

2 slices Black Forest ham or your favorite ham

1 oz Brie cheese

1 tsp Hot & Sweet Mustard or Aioli Garlic Mustard Sauce

¼ crisp apple such as Granny Smith or Honeycrisp, thinly sliced

1 Slice baguette open. Toast if desired (or toast after adding Brie cheese).

2 Spread mustard on bread. Add ham, cheese, and apples to assemble sandwich.

Prep time: 5 minutes
Serves 1

Variation: Use fig butter instead of apples

Nutrition Snapshot
*Per sandwich: 367 calories, 10 g fat, 6 g saturated fat,
25 g protein, 49 g carbs, 3 g fiber, 4 g sugar, 1126 mg sodium*

Vegetarian
Omit ham. Brie and apple combo is delicious on its own

Gluten Free
Use gluten-free bread

Arugula and Peas Pasta Salad

Pesto and pasta make a winning combination that is popular for potlucks because of its versatility and wide appeal. We like adding fresh greens like arugula to brighten up this pasta salad. Peas and mozzarella balls round out the pasta, adding flavor, color, and fun shapes.

Half (16-oz) pkg penne or any shape pasta

1 (7-oz) container refrigerated Genova Pesto

Half (7-oz) bag arugula or baby spinach

1 cup peas, cooked

1 (8-oz) pkg Ciliegine mozzarella balls

1 Cook pasta in salted water according to package directions. It makes a big difference in flavor if you salt the water, so don't skip this step.

2 When pasta is cooked, drain. Immediately add pesto and stir until pasta is coated.

3 Add remaining ingredients and stir to combine. The heat from the pasta will slightly wilt arugula leaves.

Prep and cooking time: 15 minutes
Serves 4

Nutrition Snapshot

Per serving: 595 calories, 38 g fat, 11 g saturated fat,
25 g protein, 50 g carbs, 6 g fiber, 3 g sugar, 179 mg sodium

Use gluten-free pasta

Ahi Steaks with Wasabi Sauce

The trick to preparing ahi tuna is to cook it as little as possible. Please resist the temptation to overcook! A very quick searing on each side is the way to go, making it the perfect meal for the busy person who only has a few minutes to cook. For best results, buy the freshest tuna you can get your hands on. For a pretty presentation, serve on a bed of greens.

1 lb ahi or albacore tuna steaks, thawed in milk if frozen (see tip below)

4 tsp Soyaki teriyaki sauce or soy sauce, divided

Juice of ½ lemon (1 Tbsp lemon juice)

2 Tbsp Wasabi Mayonnaise

½ tsp black pepper

½ tsp olive oil

1   Combine 2 tsp Soyaki and lemon in medium bowl. Add tuna and toss to coat. Marinate for 30 minutes.

2   Whisk wasabi mayonnaise and remaining 2 tsp Soyaki to make dipping sauce. Set aside.

3   Drain tuna and discard used marinade. Pat tuna dry with a paper towel; drying will make it brown better when cooking. Sprinkle with pepper.

4   Heat oil in skillet over medium-high heat. Cook tuna 1 minute per side for medium-rare, or 90 seconds per side for medium. Do not overcook! Fish will continue cooking after it's removed from heat, so undercook it slightly.

5   Drizzle with wasabi sauce, or serve on the side as a dip.

Prep and cooking time: 10 minutes (not including marinating time)
Serves 4

Tip: Thaw frozen fish in milk. Milk draws out the frozen taste and provides a fresh-caught flavor. If you're using fresh fish and it smells fishy, soak in milk for 1 hour in the fridge.

Nutrition Snapshot

Per serving: 192 calories, 8 g fat, 1 g saturated fat,
27 g protein, 2 g carbs, 0 g fiber, 1 g sugar, 243 mg sodium

Gluten Free

Use tamari instead
of Soyaki

Mexican Tortilla Pizza

When Wona first moved to California and camped out on her brother's couch, they practically lived on thin-crust pizzas at Pazzia, a small family-owned restaurant around the corner. For years after, they would reminisce about the best thin-crust pizzas they had ever had. Wona improvised and discovered how easy it is to make pseudo thin-crust pizzas using tortillas. The kids declared these pizzas a winning success! We love the nutty flavor and texture of Alvarado St Bakery's sprouted wheat tortillas, available on the West coast. We made a Tex-Mex version in this recipe, but you can use any pizza fixings you have on hand.

For each pizza:

1 large tortilla
¼ cup refried beans
⅓ cup shredded cheese, such as Fancy Shredded Mexican Blend
2 rounded Tbsp refrigerated Pico de Gallo, chopped tomatoes, or your favorite salsa

1 Preheat oven to 400° F.

2 Spread beans evenly on tortilla. Sprinkle with cheese. Dot with Pico de Gallo.

3 For a crisper crust, place pizzas directly on oven rack. For softer crust, place pizzas on a baking sheet. Bake for 7-9 minutes or until edges are lightly browned and cheese is melted.

Prep time: 5 minutes
Hands-off cooking time: 7-9 minutes
Serves 1

Variations: For a Greek theme, use Eggplant Garlic Spread with feta cheese and roasted bell peppers.

Nutrition Snapshot
Per pizza: 327 calories, 9 g fat, 4 g saturated fat, 21 g protein, 44 g carbs, 9 g fiber, 2 g sugar, 867 mg sodium

Substitute brown rice tortilla and monitor closely to prevent burning

Rusty Chicken

Suzanne Schroeder of Granite Bay, CA, shares her simplified version of this popular recipe. It's a family favorite she makes nearly every week. The dish gets its name from the color of the marinade, and it's the secret sauce that keeps the chicken moist, even when cooked on the grill. You can use boneless as well as bone-in chicken.

2 lbs boneless skinless chicken breast or thighs

1 ½ Tbsp maple syrup

2 Tbsp reduced sodium or regular soy sauce

3 Tbsp rice vinegar

2 Tbsp reduced fat or regular mayonnaise

1 In a bowl, whisk together all ingredients except chicken. Add chicken and turn over to coat well. Cover and refrigerate for at least half hour and up to overnight.

2 Drain and discard used marinade.
To grill: heat grill to medium-low. Place chicken on grill and cook for 5-8 minutes per side, or until cooked through and juices run clear.
To bake: Preheat oven to 400° F. Bake for 25 minutes or until cooked through and juices run clear.

Prep time: 5 minutes
Hands-off cooking time: 15-25 minutes
Serves 4

Nutrition Snapshot

Per serving: 267 calories, 3 g fat, 1 g saturated fat,
53 g protein, 2 g carbs, 0 g fiber, 2 g sugar, 235 mg sodium

Use tamari
instead of soy
sauce

Poached Salmon with Mango Salsa

Poaching is the safest way to cook salmon because there is absolutely no way you can overcook using this method. Don't be tempted to peek while the salmon is cooking: that will release the steam, which is the heat cooking the salmon. This method is similar to sous-vide cooking, where food is sealed in airtight plastic bags and submerged in a water bath. What's different is that you need not spend any money on fancy sous-vide machines! Poached salmon is very moist but bland, so we top it with flavorful pesto and a fruity salsa. If you are really trying to impress, splurge on King salmon.

2 (6-oz) salmon fillets, thawed if frozen

2 Tbsp refrigerated Genova Pesto

½ cup refrigerated Tropical Mango Pineapple Salsa, or your favorite salsa

Half onion, lemon slices, or bay leaves to flavor poaching water

1 Choose a saucepan that will hold enough water to completely cover salmon fillets. Fill with enough water to cover salmon (1 ½ inches or more, depending on thickness of fillets), adding any desired seasonings such as onion, lemon, or bay leaves. Bring water to a boil over high heat.

2 Add salmon skin-side down and cover pan so steam cannot escape. Turn off heat.

3 Let salmon steam for 8-10 minutes per inch of thickness, or until water is completely cooled. It is impossible to overcook since there is no flame!

4 Remove salmon from water and remove skin; it should come off easily. Flip right side up and spread with pesto. Top with salsa.

Prep time: 5 minutes
Hands-off cooking time: 10-15 minutes, can be left much longer
Serves 2

Nutrition Snapshot

Per serving: 444 calories, 29 g fat, 6 g saturated fat,
35 g protein, 8 g carbs, 1 g fiber, 6 g sugar, 324 mg sodium

Gluten Free

Lavash Pizza Pinwheels

For a fun twist on traditional pepperoni pizza, try using Middle Eastern lavash to create rolled pizzas. The kids will love making their own. We went light on the pepperoni to control sodium. Throw on any pizza toppings you like!

For each rollup:

1 sheet lavash, regular or whole wheat

¼ cup jarred Pizza Sauce or your favorite marinara sauce

½ cup shredded mozzarella cheese

6 slices pepperoni (optional)

1 Preheat oven to 350° F. Line a baking sheet with parchment paper or a silicone baking mat.

2 Spread pizza sauce evenly on lavash. Don't use too much sauce, or it will ooze out when you're cutting the rolls. Sprinkle with cheese. Dot with pepperoni.

3 Beginning with one of the short ends, roll into a log and place seam side down on baking sheet.

4 Bake for 15 minutes until cheese is melted.

5 Remove from heat and let cool for 5 minutes before slicing into pinwheels.

Prep time: 5 minutes
Cooking time: 15 minutes
Serves 1

Nutrition Snapshot

Per roll-up: 480 calories, 16 g fat, 7 g saturated fat, 26 g protein, 61 g carbs, 7 g fiber, 6 g sugar, 940 mg sodium

Omit pepperoni

Gyoza Stir Fry

Gyoza, also known as potstickers, are delicious dumplings, available frozen at Trader Joe's and filled with your pick of chicken, pork, shrimp, or veggies. We pan-fried these little morsels and added bagged stir fry veggies to create a colorful one-meal bowl overflowing with broccoli, peppers, snap peas, snow peas, onions, mushrooms, carrots, bok choy, bamboo shoots, baby corn, and water chestnuts. If substituting your own vegetables, use 4 cups of any vegetables you have on hand.

1 (16-oz) bag frozen gyoza or potstickers, any flavor

1 Tbsp olive oil

1 (18-oz) pkg refrigerated Asian Style Stir Fry vegetables, or 3 cups vegetables

⅓ cup water

⅓ cup Gyoza Dipping Sauce or Soyaki teriyaki sauce

1 Heat oil over medium high heat in a large skillet or wok. Place frozen gyoza in pan and cook for

2 minutes until edges are browned and crisp.

3 Add vegetables and water. Immediately cover pan and let steam 5 minutes, or until water has evaporated.

4 Add sauce and toss until combined. Use a spatula to loosen any stubborn gyoza that may be stuck to the pan.

Prep and cooking time: 10 minutes
Serves 4

Nutrition Snapshot
Per serving: 238 calories, 8 g fat, 1 g saturated fat, 9 g protein, 30 g carbs, 5 g fiber, 6 g sugar, 937 mg sodium

Vegetarian

Use vegetarian gyoza

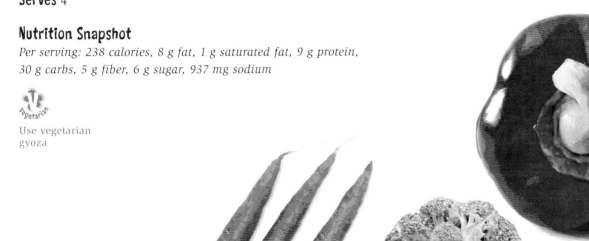

4 Sides

Bacon and Chive Mashed Potatoes

Basic mashed potatoes get depth and zing from bacon and chives in this recipe. Use Russet potatoes since they are high in starch and make the fluffiest mashed potatoes. Many recipes ask you to peel and cube the potatoes beforehand in order to speed up boiling time. However that only creates a lot of work, resulting in dense mashed potatoes since cubed potatoes tend to absorb a lot of water as they boil. Boil them whole, then slip the skins off after boiling – much easier than peeling raw potatoes.

2 pounds russet potatoes (about 4 potatoes)

2 Tbsp butter, cold (do not melt beforehand)

½ tsp salt

¼ tsp black pepper

½ cup milk, warmed

2 strips Fully Cooked Bacon, crisped and crumbled

1 Tbsp finely chopped fresh chives, plus extra for garnish

1 Wash potatoes (do not peel yet). Place potatoes in a pot, cover with water, and bring to a boil. Cook potatoes for 30 minutes or until tender (poke with a knife). Drain.

2 Slip potato skins off using your fingers. Run under cold water if potatoes are too hot to handle. Place peeled potatoes in a large bowl.

3 While potatoes are hot, add butter, salt, pepper, and milk. Mash together until combined. Add more milk if necessary to get desired consistency; potatoes will thicken as they cool. Stir in bacon and chives. Taste and adjust seasoning. Garnish with chives.

Prep time: 5-10 minutes
Hands-off cooking time: 30-40 minutes
Serves 4

Nutrition Snapshot
Per serving: 242 calories, 8 g fat, 5 g saturated fat,
6 g protein, 37 g carbs, 5 g fiber, 4 g sugar, 390 mg sodium

Vegetarian G Gluten Free

Omit bacon or substitute vegetarian bacon

Scallion Fried Rice

Fried rice is a common staple of Asian cuisine. There are countless variations using all kinds of meats, vegetables, and sauces. This one is the most basic, flavored with just scallions (green onions), eggs, salt, and pepper. Add any leftover meats or veggies you have on hand; just finely dice and add to the mix.

2 cups cooked rice (brown or white, available precooked in freezer case)

4 scallions, chopped

2 eggs, beaten

1 Tbsp olive oil

½ tsp salt

¼ tsp black pepper

1 Heat oil in a wok or skillet over medium-high heat. Add scallions and cook 30 seconds.

2 Combine rice and eggs in a bowl, mixing until rice is evenly coated with egg. Add rice to wok and cook for another 3 minutes, stirring occasionally, until rice is warmed throughout.

3 Sprinkle with salt and pepper, and toss to combine. Check for seasonings and serve.

Prep and cooking time: 10 minutes
Serves 4

Tip: Leftover rice (stored in fridge) works well in fried rice recipes.

Nutrition Snapshot

Per serving: 192 calories, 6 g fat, 1 g saturated fat, 5 g protein, 29 g carbs, 2 g fiber, 1 g sugar, 328 mg sodium

Sweet and Spicy Corn and Tomato Medley

We are in love with Trader Joe's Corn and Chile tomato-less salsa. It's sweet, spicy, and packed with flavor. Guess what we did to this tomato-less salsa: We added tomatoes, of course! Combining this yummy salsa with fresh tomatoes, pinto beans, diced avocado, and crispy cucumber makes a winning side dish.

1 (13.75-oz) jar Corn and Chile salsa

1 cup halved cherry or grape tomatoes

1 (15-oz) can pinto beans, drained and rinsed

1 ripe avocado, diced

3 Persian cucumbers, diced (no need to peel)

1 Add all ingredients to a serving bowl; stir gently to combine.

Prep time: 5 minutes
Serves 4

Nutrition Snapshot

Per serving: 253 calories, 5 g fat, 1 g saturated fat, 8 g protein, 28 g carbs, 11 g fiber, 2 g sugar, 329 mg sodium

Oven Roasted Teeny Tiny Potatoes

You are so cute I'm going to eat you up! Trader Joe's carries bags of adorable Teeny Tiny Potatoes that are irresistible. These itty bitty oven roasted potatoes are delicious—crispy, golden, and seasoned on the outside, soft and moist on the inside. Olive oil helps the potatoes roast in the pan, but don't worry about your waistline since much of the oil stays in the pan. If you can't find Teeny Tiny Potatoes, you can use fingerling potatoes, which are just a tad larger and a bit jealous.

1 (16-oz) bag Teeny Tiny Potatoes or fingerling potatoes

2 Tbsp olive oil

½ tsp salt

¼ tsp black pepper

2 cloves garlic, crushed, or 2 cubes frozen Crushed Garlic

3-4 sprigs fresh rosemary

1 Preheat oven to 400° F.

2 Wash potatoes but do not peel. Pat potatoes dry.

3 In a large bowl, mix together oil, salt, pepper, garlic, and whole rosemary sprigs. If using frozen garlic cubes, let thaw in bowl before mixing. Add potatoes to bowl and stir until well coated.

4 Empty potatoes (scraping oil and seasonings out as well) onto baking sheet, spreading potatoes out evenly. Bake for 35-40 minutes, using metal spatula to flip and move pieces halfway through baking time. Discard rosemary springs when serving.

Prep time: 10 minutes
Hands-off cooking time: 40 minutes
Serves 4

Variation: Roast sweet potatoes chunks using this same method.

Nutrition Snapshot

Per serving: 160 calories, 8 g fat, 1 g saturated fat,
2 g protein, 19 g carbs, 3 g fiber, 1 g sugar, 330 mg sodium

Vegetarian Gluten Free

Middle-Eastern Dill Rice

Dill rice is a favorite in Persian cooking, and it goes well with lemony dishes, chicken, or fish. We use fluffy long-grain basmati rice, adding onions, butter, and fresh dill for flavor.

1 cup basmati rice

1 Tbsp olive oil

1 Tbsp butter

½ cup chopped onion

1 clove garlic, crushed or 1 cube frozen Crushed Garlic

¼ tsp salt

¼ cup chopped fresh dill

1 Add oil and butter to a saucepan over. Add onion; cook and stir for 5 minutes until onions are soft. Add garlic and sauté for 1 minute more.

2 Add rice, 1 ¾ cup water, and salt. Stir briefly to combine. Bring to a boil and simmer over low heat for 15-20 minutes or until water is absorbed. Fluff rice and stir in dill. Cover and steam for 1 minute more.

Prep time: 5 minutes
Cooking time: 20-25 minutes (mostly hands off)
Serves 4

Nutrition Snapshot
Per serving: 232 calories, 7 g fat, 2 g saturated fat, 3 g protein, 39 g carbs, 1 g fiber, 1 g sugar, 147 mg sodium

Vegetarian   Gluten Free

Carrot Pasta

Carrot pasta is the specialty of Deana's 11-year-old daughter, Layla, who has made it for years. The original method was to get a bag of whole carrots and use a vegetable peeler to cut the carrots into long, wide ribbons. It takes a looong time, and Layla would sit and patiently turn the entire bag of carrots into a bowl of ribbons. You can use the Layla method, or you can substitute a bag of Trader Joe's pre-shredded carrots and spend the extra time playing card games with the kids.

1 (10-oz) bag Shredded Carrots
Few sprigs rosemary
1 Tbsp butter
¼ tsp salt
¼ tsp black pepper

1 Melt butter in a wide saucepan or skillet over medium high heat. Add carrots and rosemary; sprinkle with salt and pepper.

2 Once carrots are heated through, lower heat to medium-low; cook and stir for about 5 minutes until carrots are tender but not mushy. Discard rosemary or use as garnish.

Prep and cooking time: 8 minutes
Serves 6

Nutrition Snapshot
Per serving: 35 calories, 2 g fat, 1 g saturated fat, 1 g protein, 4 g carbs, 1 g fiber, 3 g sugar, 129 mg sodium

Vegetarian Gluten Free

Minted Quinoa

Quinoa is a protein-packed seed that is generally cooked, used, and served in the same ways as rice. We cook the quinoa in chicken broth for extra flavor, and then stir in sun-dried tomatoes and fresh mint. The simple secret to great taste? The oil used to pack the sun-dried tomatoes is very flavorful and adds delicious richness to the quinoa.

1 cup uncooked quinoa (any combination of red, white, or tricolor quinoa)

2 cups chicken broth

⅓ cup Julienne Sliced Sun Dried Tomatoes (with the oil)

½ cup chopped fresh mint

1 Rinse quinoa before cooking; this will remove the natural bitterness.

2 Add quinoa and broth to a saucepan. Bring to a boil and simmer over low heat for 15 minutes or until liquid is absorbed and quinoa is tender.

3 Stir in sun-dried tomato and mint.

Prep time: 5 minutes
Hands-off cooking time: 15 minutes
Serves 4

Helpful Tip: Start every quinoa recipe by rinsing and draining the quinoa. Quinoa can have a bitter soapy coating that should be rinsed before using.

Nutrition Snapshot
Per serving: 226 calories, 7 g fat, 1 g saturated fat,
6 g protein, 35 g carbs, 4 g fiber, 4 g sugar, 296 mg sodium

Use
vegetable
broth

Use gluten-free
chicken broth

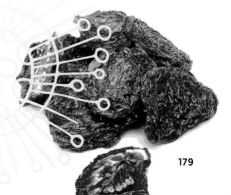

Roasted Carrots and Fennel with Parmesan

When carrots and fennel are roasted, their flavors transform, becoming sweeter, nuttier, and caramelized. These roasted roots are a fantastic side dish to heartier main meals such as beef and lamb, and they are ideal for any autumn meal. Vegetarians will appreciate the richness of roasted root vegetables paired with creamy mains such as risotto. Experiment by adding more root vegetables such as beets, turnips, and parsnips. (Use a second pan or cut back the amount of fennel and carrots).

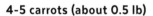

4-5 carrots (about 0.5 lb)

2 large bulbs fennel (about 1.25 lbs)

2 Tbsp olive oil

¼ tsp salt

¼ tsp black pepper

2 Tbsp shaved or shredded Parmesan cheese

1 Preheat oven to 400° F.

2 Slice fennel bulbs ½ inch thick. Slice carrots lengthwise so that the thickness is ½ inch or less. Cut carrot into shorter pieces.

3 Place carrots and fennel on baking sheet and drizzle with oil. Toss to coat well. Sprinkle with salt and pepper and toss again. Spread vegetables evenly.

4 Roast in oven for 45 minutes, flipping vegetables halfway through cooking time.

5 When serving, sprinkle with Parmesan.

Prep time: 10 minutes
Hands-off cooking time: 45 minutes
Serves 4

Nutrition Snapshot

Per serving: 128 calories, 8 g fat, 2 g saturated fat, 3 g protein, 14 g carbs, 5 g fiber, 3 g sugar, 269 mg sodium

Potatoes Au Gratin

This dish is traditionally made with heavy cream to create a thick cheesy sauce for the potatoes. We make a lighter version using chicken broth and think it's just as delicious. Try adding bacon crumbles or breadcrumbs on top for extra flavor and texture.

2 lbs potatoes (we prefer red or Yukon gold, but Russet can also be used), peeled and thinly sliced about ⅛-inch thick

1 small onion, thinly sliced (optional)

1 tsp salt

½ tsp black pepper

¼ tsp nutmeg (optional)

1 ¼ cups chicken broth

1 cup shredded cheese, such as Swiss & Gruyère blend

1 Preheat oven to 400° F. Lightly grease a 9x13-inch baking pan or casserole dish.

2 In a bowl, combine sliced potatoes, onion, salt, pepper, and nutmeg. Stir to coat.

3 Arrange potato mixture in baking dish and spread evenly. Pour broth over potatoes. Sprinkle cheese evenly on top. Spray underside of aluminum foil with oil and cover dish, pulling back one corner to let steam escape.

4 Bake for 1 hour. For a golden brown top, remove foil for last 15 minutes, or broil for a few minutes just before serving.

Prep time: 20 minutes
Hands-off cooking time: 1 hour
Serves 6

Variation: Try making this dish with sweet potatoes.

Nutrition Snapshot

Per serving: 213 calories, 6 g fat, 3 g saturated fat, 9 g protein, 28 g carbs, 3 g fiber, 1 g sugar, 451 mg sodium

Use vegetable broth   Use gluten-free chicken broth

Springtime Spinach Rice

Wona tried a similar dish at a vegetarian Chinese restaurant and loved it so much she had to recreate it at home. A couple of rounds with the recipe taught her that only fresh spinach gives pale rice a bright green color. You can use frozen spinach and it will taste great, but it will be a darker duller color and the rice won't be green. For a speedy complete meal, top with a fried egg.

1 (6-oz) bag spinach, finely chopped in food processor, or half (10-oz) pkg frozen spinach, thawed and excess water squeezed out

2 Tbsp olive oil

1 small onion, finely chopped

2 cups cooked rice (brown or white, available precooked in freezer case)

¼ cup toasted pine nuts

½ tsp salt

1 Heat oil in wok or skillet over medium heat. Add onion; cook and stir for 2-3 minutes until softened. Add spinach and cook 2-3 minutes longer.

2 Add rice, pine nuts, and salt. Cook 5 minutes, stirring frequently, until rice is heated through.

Prep and cooking time: 15 minutes   **Serves** 4

Nutrition Snapshot

Per serving: 220 calories, 8 g fat,
1 g saturated fat, 4 g protein, 33 g carbs,
6 g fiber, 1 g sugar, 341 mg sodium

Black Bean Mango Tango

The flavor and texture of this black-bean-powered side dish will have you doing a happy dance. Sweet mango and sweet corn balance Trader Joe's tangy Cilantro Salad Dressing; cucumber adds crunch and freshness. If you don't love cilantro, you might want to give this dressing a chance as it doesn't have an overpowering cilantro flavor. If you do love cilantro, chop some extra up and add it on top!

1 cup diced mango

1 (15-oz) can black beans, drained and rinsed

1 (15.25-oz) can corn, drained

2 Persian cucumbers, diced (no need to peel)

½ cup refrigerated Cilantro Salad Dressing

¼ tsp salt

1   Add all ingredients to a serving bowl; stir to gently combine.

Prep time: 5-10 minutes
Serves 4

Nutrition Snapshot

Per serving: 227 calories, 5 g fat, 1 g saturated fat, 10 g protein, 35 g carbs, 7 g fiber, 13 g sugar, 534 mg sodium

 Vegetarian   Gluten Free

Quinoa Tabbouleh

The bright fresh flavors of this Middle Eastern salad have made it a favorite the world over. We use protein-packed quinoa in place of traditional bulgur, and taste-testers hardly noticed the difference. If you have tomatoes and/or cucumbers on hand, they make nice additions to this salad. Feta cheese also goes well.

1 cup uncooked quinoa

Juice and zest of 2 lemons

¼ cup olive oil

1 garlic clove, crushed, or 1 cube frozen Crushed Garlic

1 cup chopped fresh parsley

1 cup cherry tomatoes, halved (optional)

½ tsp salt, divided

½ tsp black pepper

1 Rinse quinoa before cooking; this will remove the natural bitterness.

2 Place quinoa in a pot with 2 cups water and ¼ tsp salt. Cook on high heat until water comes to a boil. Reduce heat to low; cover and cook for 15-20 minutes or until liquid has been absorbed. Fluff with a fork.

3 Combine cooked quinoa with remaining ingredients. The flavors meld and improve if the tabbouleh sits at room temperature for a few hours.

Prep time: 10 minutes
Hands-off cooking time (for quinoa): 15 minutes
Serves 6

Nutrition Snapshot
Per serving: 155 calories, 6 g fat, 1 g saturated fat, 5 g protein, 21 g carbs, 3 g fiber, 1 g sugar, 201 mg sodium

Vegetarian   Gluten Free

5 Desserts & Drinks

Peanut Butter Cup Pudding

Once upon a time, peanut butter met chocolate, and they lived happily ever after. This classic and familiar flavor combination shines in this pudding dessert. Homemade peanut butter pudding is layered with rich Belgian chocolate pudding, homage to the ever-popular peanut butter cup. If desired, top with whipped cream, and garnish with some of Trader Joe's mini peanut butter cups for a cute presentation.

½ cup creamy salted peanut butter

1 ½ cups whole milk

¼ cup sugar

2 Tbsp cornstarch

1 (16-oz) tub Belgian Chocolate Pudding

1 Combine milk, sugar, and cornstarch in a saucepan over medium heat. Bring to a boil; lower heat and continue to cook until thick (about 10 minutes), stirring constantly.

2 Add peanut butter and whisk until smooth. Divide pudding between 6 glasses. Cover with plastic wrap and chill in refrigerator for 2 hours.

3 Top peanut butter layer with ⅓ cup chocolate pudding.

Prep and cooking time: 15 minutes (not including chill time)
Serves 6

Nutrition Snapshot

Per serving: 374 calories, 22 g fat, 7 g saturated fat,
10 g protein, 40 g carbs, 3 g fiber, 30 g sugar, 184 mg sodium

Vegetarian Gluten Free

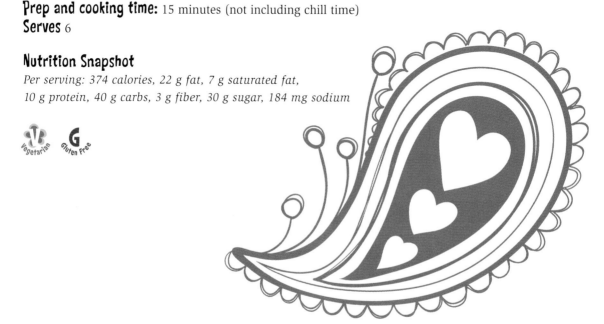

Lemon Blueberry Tart

Lemon curd is an English specialty spread, creamy and tangy. It's very rich, so it's often paired with fresh fruit or pastry to balance lemon curd's intense flavor and texture. For an easy tart, spread the lemon curd on a cooked pastry crust and top with fresh berries (and even ice cream or whipped cream). This tart will last just fine in the fridge and can be made a few hours ahead of time. Keep a jar of lemon curd in the pantry and a pie crust in the freezer, ready to go as a last minute dessert. If the Queen drops by for high tea, you'll be prepared. Is Trader Joe's out of lemon curd? Don't worry—try our 10-minute Lemon Curd recipe on page 214.

1 frozen pie crust, thawed

1 (10.5-oz) jar Lemon Curd or 1 ½ cups lemon curd

1 cup heavy cream

1 Tbsp sugar

2 cups fresh blueberries

1 Place crust in tart pan or pie dish and press dough up the sides about ½ inch.

2 Bake crust according to package instructions.

3 Remove crust from oven and cool completely. Spread lemon curd in an even layer across bottom of crust.

4 In a large bowl, beat cream and sugar together until whipped cream forms peaks.

5 Add layer of whipped cream to tart and top with blueberries. Chill for later, or serve right away.

Prep and cooking time: 15 minutes (not counting cooling time)
Yield: 8 servings

Nutrition Snapshot

Per serving: 580 calories, 33 g fat, 13 g saturated fat,
5 g protein, 71 g carbs, 3 g fiber, 55 g sugar, 90 mg sodium

Use gluten-free pie crust
available at other grocers

Stovetop Crème Brulee

Crème brulee is a custard named for the burnt sugar layer on top that cracks and crunches satisfyingly as you push in your spoon. Most of us see crème brulee on the menus of fancy restaurants and assume it must fall in the domain of trained expert chefs. Be intimidated no more! It so happens that crème brulee is a dessert of few ingredients—cream, egg yolks, sugar, and vanilla. This simple recipe skips all the oven steps (involving a water bath) and does it all on the stovetop. It has a little more tooth (denseness) than oven-cooked crème brulees, but if anyone asks, you can say the stovetop version is the original way to make this classic, elegant dessert.

2 cups (16 fl oz) heavy cream

4 egg yolks

¼ cup sugar plus extra sugar for the top

2 tsp vanilla extract

1 Heat cream in a saucepan over medium heat until hot but not boiling, about 2-3 minutes. Remove from heat.

2 In a large bowl, whisk together egg yolks, sugar, and vanilla. Pour in hot cream, a little at a time, while whisking. Pour mixture back into saucepan and whisk over medium-low heat until thickened, about 6-7 minutes. Lower heat if mixture begins to bubble.

3 Divide mixture among 6 ramekins and chill in fridge for 3 hours (or until the next day).

4 To make the burnt sugar crust, evenly sprinkle each custard with about 2 tsp sugar and use a blowtorch or kitchen torch to melt it until the sugar looks glossy. Let it rest 5 minutes before serving so that the rim can cool.

Prep and cooking time: about 15 minutes (not including time to chill or to torch the crust)
Serves 6

Helpful tip: For best results, create the burnt sugar crust in two phases: melt the sugar partway so that it bubbles up, wait one minute, then torch it a second time to melt sugar the rest of the way.

Nutrition Snapshot
Per serving: 339 calories, 35 g fat, 17 g saturated fat, 2 g protein,
9 g carbs, 0 g fiber, 9 g sugar, 32 mg sodium

Strawberry Coconut Smoothie

This smoothie will make you feel good inside and out, promises health food blogger Jennifer Drummond (PeanutButterAndPeppers.com) who created this low-calorie, refreshing drink. It's the perfect smoothie to quench your thirst after a workout or if you're feeling dehydrated. Coconut water has fewer calories, less sodium, and more potassium than a sports drink. Drink up!

- 1 ¼ cup coconut water
- 1 cup strawberries, frozen
- 1 tsp honey (add more if you like a sweeter smoothie)

1 Add all ingredients in a blender and blend until smooth.

Prep time: 5 minutes   **Serves** 1

Nutrition Snapshot
Per serving: 154 calories, 0 g fat, 0 g saturated fat, 4 g protein, 36 g carbs, 7 g fiber, 27 g sugar, 315 mg sodium

 Vegetarian
 Gluten Free

Piña Colada (Dairy-Free) Soft Ice Cream

Drift away to a tropical paradise with this delicious frozen treat... and you'll have plenty of time to spend in paradise once you get there because this recipe takes only a few minutes! You don't need an ice cream maker to make ice cream at home. Instead, use a food processor to make healthy soft ice cream simply by blending frozen fruit with cream or coconut milk.

1 (16-oz) bag frozen Pineapple Tidbits
1 cup canned light coconut milk
¼ cup sugar

1   Combine coconut milk and sugar in a bowl, stirring 15 seconds until sugar starts to dissolve.

2   Do not thaw pineapple. For this recipe it should be frozen hard. Add frozen pineapple and coconut mixture to a food processor. Process for approximately 2 minutes or until mixture is smooth. Serve immediately.

Prep time: 5-10 minutes   **Serves** 4

Nutrition Snapshot
Per serving: 161 calories, 3 g fat, 2 g saturated fat, 0 g protein, 32 g carbs, 2 g fiber, 28 g sugar, 19 mg sodium

Vegetarian   Gluten Free

Fleur de Sel Caramel Buns

These sticky buns are covered in pecans and caramel, with a touch of cinnamon. They're baked together and pulled apart for individual servings. Canned biscuits and caramel sauce make this recipe more of an assembly than actual cooking. But you don't have to let on to your guests.

1 (16-oz) can Buttermilk Biscuits (8 biscuits)
¼ cup jarred Fleur de Sel Caramel Sauce
⅓ cup chopped pecans
¼ cup sugar
1 tsp cinnamon

1 Preheat oven to 350° F.

2 Butter an 8-inch round cake pan or pie dish. Spread caramel sauce on the bottom, and sprinkle with pecans.

3 Combine sugar and cinnamon in a bowl.

4 Separate biscuit dough and toss each piece in cinnamon-sugar mixture, coating all sides. Place dough pieces in pan. Pour extra sugar-cinnamon mixture over the top.

5 Bake for 30 minutes. Immediately invert pan onto serving dish and let caramel run down onto buns. If any of the caramel or pecans sticks to the pan, scrape off and drop onto buns. (Do not let buns cool in pan; otherwise it will be hard to remove once caramel cools.) Immediately fill empty pan with water to make washing easier.

Prep time: 10 minutes
Hands-off cooking time: 30 minutes
Serves 8

Nutrition Snapshot
Per serving: 270 calories, 12 g fat, 6 g saturated fat, 5 g protein,
38 g carbs, 1 g fiber, 16 g sugar, 488 mg sodium

Italian Almond Cookies

These cookies are slightly chewy on the outside and have a moist and dense marzipan-like center. There is no flour, only ground almonds, so the delicious flavor of sweetened almonds has the spotlight, with just a touch of vanilla. Pine nuts decorate the top and add another layer of gourmet flavor, but for a more budget-friendly alternative, slivered almonds can be substituted.

2 ½ cups almond meal

2 egg whites

½ cup sugar

1 tsp vanilla extract

⅓ cup toasted pine nuts

1 Preheat oven to 350° F.

2 Whisk together egg whites, sugar, and vanilla.

3 Stir almond meal in one cup at a time. The dough will be sticky.

4 Place pine nuts in a shallow dish. Take tablespoonfuls of dough, use hands to roll into a ball, and press tops into pine nuts. Use a tapping motion to embed pine nuts in dough. Place on baking sheet lined with parchment paper or a Silpat baking mat. Space cookies by about 1 inch – they will not spread much as they bake.

5 Bake for 15 minutes. Let cookies cool completely before removing from baking sheet.

Prep time: 10 minutes
Hands-off cooking time: 15 minutes
Makes 20 cookies

Nutrition Snapshot

Per cookie: 124 calories, 9 g fat, 1 g saturated fat, 4 g protein,
8 g carbs, 2 g fiber, 6 g sugar, 6 mg sodium

Tip: When rolling sticky cookie dough into balls, make sure your hands are clean. If dough sticks to your hands, wet your hands slightly and the dough will not stick.

Flourless Peanut Butter Cookies

These easy peanut butter cookies are sweet, dense, nutty, and slightly chewy, just the way they should be, all without the flour. You can substitute other nut butters such as sunflower butter or cashew butter for adventurous variations. Add chocolate chips, cinnamon, or cayenne pepper for a little kick.

1 (16-oz) jar creamy salted peanut butter (about 1 ¾ cups) at room temperature

1 cup sugar

2 eggs

1 tsp vanilla extract

1 Preheat oven to 350° F.

2 In a medium bowl, mix together peanut butter, sugar, eggs, and vanilla until smooth. Dough will start to thicken as it is being mixed together.

3 Scoop walnut-size portions of dough, lightly roll in hands, and place on a lightly oiled or lined baking sheet (Silpat baking mats work well). Dough will be soft but it holds together without being sticky. Place cookies about 1-2 inches apart, as they will not spread much.

4 Flatten cookies with tines of a fork, making traditional crosshatch imprints on top of cookies. If fork sticks, wipe tines clean in between cookies.

5 Bake for 12 minutes or until edges are golden and cookie is still soft. Don't overbake these cookies! Cool cookies before removing from baking sheet.

Prep time: 10 minutes
Hands-off cooking time: 12 minutes
Makes 30 cookies

Nutrition Snapshot

Per cookie: 120 calories, 8 g fat, 1 g saturated fat, 4 g protein, 10 g carbs, 1 g fiber, 7 g sugar, 70 mg sodium

Vegetarian

Gluten Free

Chocolate Cherry Challah Bread Pudding

Holla for Challah! This delicious bread pudding is made with sweet challah bread soaked in liquid brownie mix and topped with sweet-tart cherries. Trader Joe's powdered brownie mix is simply combined with whole milk—no other ingredients are needed. Prep this dish beforehand, popping it into the oven during the main meal. By the time it's cooked, you'll be ready for dessert, and dessert will be ready for you.

1 ¼ cups (½ the 16-oz pkg) Brownie Truffle Baking Mix (dry mix only; don't add anything else)

2 cups whole milk

¾ of a (12-oz) loaf Challah bread, diced into ½-inch cubes (about 6 cups)

½ cup Dried Pitted Tart Montmorency Cherries

Vanilla ice cream or whipped cream (optional)

1 Place diced bread in 8x8-inch lightly greased or buttered baking dish and arrange so dish is filled evenly. Scatter cherries over the top.

2 In a bowl, combine milk and brownie mix. Stir well for a minute until dissolved. There are chocolate chips in the mixture—don't worry about those. Pour this mixture over the diced bread, scattering chocolate chips across the top. Lightly press down on bread pieces so that they are all soaked through with brownie liquid.

3 Set aside pan while you preheat oven to 350° F, about 10 minutes. This extra time will give the bread time to soak further. Cover pan tightly with foil and bake for about 30 minutes. Remove foil and bake an additional 10 minutes uncovered.

4 Remove pan from oven and let it cool for 15 minutes, allowing bread pudding to set. Serve warm with vanilla ice cream or whipped cream.

Note: This recipe has been designed to use a ½ package of the Brownie Truffle Mix (there are 2 ½ cups mix in each package). Save remaining mix for your next batch of bread pudding.

Prep time: 5-10 minutes
Hands-off cooking time: 30 minutes
Serves 8

Nutrition Snapshot
Per serving: 392 calories, 15 g fat, 6 g saturated fat,
6 g protein, 56 g carbs, 3 g fiber, 27 g sugar, 340 mg sodium

Simple Apple Tart

A remarkably beautiful tart, irresistible in its simplicity and absolutely delicious! Try this sophisticated version of apple pie. For a fancy touch, warm some apricot jam (to make it easier to spread) and brush on top of cooked tart for a delectable sheen.

1 pie crust, thawed
3 large or 4 medium Golden Delicious apples
2 Tbsp sugar
2 Tbsp butter, sliced thin
2 Tbsp apricot jam, warmed (optional)

1 Preheat oven to 375° F.

2 Press pie crust into a 10-inch tart pan. Trim any excess crust. Prick evenly with a fork.

3 Peel, core, and thinly slice apples (about 1/8-inch thick). Arrange in overlapping pattern on pie crust.

4 Sprinkle sugar evenly over apples. Spread butter pieces evenly over apples.

5 Bake for 45 minutes or until apples are golden.

6 For a fancy touch, whisk apricot jam with 1 Tbsp water, warm in microwave, and brush on top of cooked tart. The jam will make the apples glisten.

Prep time: 20 minutes   **Hands-off cooking time:** 45 minutes   **Serves** 8

Nutrition Snapshot
Per serving: 274 calories, 16 g fat, 9 g saturated fat, 2 g protein, 31 g carbs, 4 g fiber, 13 g sugar, 42 mg sodium

Use gluten-free pie crust available at other grocers

Strawberry Banana Smoothie Popsicle

Jennifer Drummond, author of the popular health blog PeanutButterAndPeppers.com, shares her recipe for a healthy, guilt-free popsicle that tastes like a smoothie. It is the perfect balance of bananas, strawberries, Greek yogurt, and milk. They are a wonderful nutritious snack to give children after a long day of playing outside. If you don't have popsicle molds, you can use paper cups as molds. Popsicle sticks are sold at craft stores.

1 cup strawberries, fresh or frozen
1 banana, fresh or frozen
½ cup plain nonfat Greek yogurt
½ cup non-fat milk
1 tsp honey or sugar

1 Add all ingredients in a blender and process until smooth. Pour mixture into popsicle molds.

2 Place in freezer for approximately 6 hours or until set. If your molds don't include built-in sticks, wait about 2 hours until popsicles are partially frozen, cover with foil, cut a slit through foil, and insert popsicle sticks.

3 Run popsicle mold under warm water and pop out of mold to serve.

Prep time: 10 minutes   **Makes** 9 (4-oz) popsicles

Nutrition Snapshot

Per popsicle: 34 calories, 0 g fat, 0 g saturated fat, 2 g protein, 7 g carbs, 1 g fiber, 5 g sugar, 10 mg sodium

Vegetarian   Gluten Free

Chocolate Mousse Pie

It's hard to believe that this incredibly delicious layered dessert has only five ingredients. Silky dark chocolate mousse is topped with a creamy light chocolate topping, landing this dessert at the top of our chocolate fantasies. A pastry crust gives a nice contrasting texture, although any kind of crust can be used (prebaked, graham, or cookie crusts all work). If you serve this pie to guests, prepare to be asked for the recipe.

1 frozen pie crust, thawed, or use prebaked crust
1 (12-oz) bag semi-sweet chocolate chips
1 (14-oz) can light coconut milk
1 ½ cups heavy cream
3 Tbsp hot cocoa mix powder

Crust:

1 Preheat oven to 425° F.

2 Place pie crust in pie dish. Line with parchment paper, fill with pie weights or beans, and bake crust for 15 minutes. Remove from oven and cool completely.

Filling:

1 Melt chocolate chips in microwave. (Microwave for 1 minute and then in 30 second increments, stirring well in between until completely smooth and melted. Do not scorch.)

2 Pour coconut milk into blender. Add melted chocolate. Immediately blend until completely smooth, about 20-30 seconds. Pour filling into crust and chill for 4 hours or overnight in fridge.

Topping:

1 In a large bowl, add cream and cocoa mix. Using hand mixer, beat on high speed until stiff peaks form. Do not overmix. Top pie with whipped cream. Serve or return to fridge until ready to serve.

2 Garnish with a sprinkle of cocoa powder or berries if desired.

Helpful Tip: When cutting pie, wipe knife clean between cuts.

Prep time: 10-15 minutes (not including cooling and setting times)
Hands-off cooking time: 15 minutes
Serves 12

Nutrition Snapshot

Per serving: 406 calories, 30 g fat, 18 g saturated fat,
4 g protein, 33 g carbs, 3 g fiber, 18 g sugar, 65 mg sodium

  Use gluten-free pie crust available at other grocers

Vanilla Chai Pudding

Trader Joe's powdered chai can be used in a hot drink mix of course, but we've had fun using it in other recipes such as bread pudding (in "Cooking with Trader Joe's: Companion") and the pudding here. This pudding recipe is a traditional cornstarch pudding (you get that old-fashioned skin that forms on top) and is flavored with chai and vanilla.

4 cups whole milk

1 scoop (3 Tbsp) Spicy Chai Latte Mix

⅓ cup cornstarch

¼ cup sugar

2 tsp vanilla extract

1 Combine all ingredients in a medium saucepan (no heat) and whisk until cornstarch has completely dissolved.

2 Place saucepan over medium heat and continue stirring. After about 5 minutes, you will notice mixture starting to thicken. At this point, continue whisking constantly for another 5 minutes, lowering heat if mixture begins to boil over.

3 Immediately divide between 6 serving bowls. Enjoy warm, or refrigerate for 2 hours until pudding is set.

Prep and cooking time: 15 minutes
Serves 6

Nutrition Snapshot
Per serving: 189 calories, 6 g fat, 4 g saturated fat, 6 g protein, 29 g carbs, 0 g fiber, 22 g sugar, 76 mg sodium

Vegetarian Gluten Free

Mini Ice Cream Sandwiches

Wona's friend Gloria Lee from Oakland, CA first made these magical little ice cream sandwiches at birthday parties for her sons Corbin and Asher, and the parents ate just as many as the kids! Make them ahead of time to give the crunchy cookies time to soften. Try other variations such as Coconut Cookie Thins with chocolate ice cream, or Lemon Cookie Thins with vanilla ice cream.

For each mini sandwich:

2 Ginger Cookie Thins
2 Tbsp light or regular vanilla ice cream

1 Remove ice cream from freezer and let soften for a few minutes at room temperature.

2 Place ice cream on top of a cookie, and lightly press another cookie on top. An old-fashioned ice cream scoop is very handy here. Smooth edges as needed.

3 Store in freezer for at least 2 hours to allow ice cream to refreeze and cookies to soften.

Prep time: 5 minutes
Serves 1

Nutrition Snapshot

Per mini sandwich: 59 calories, 2 g fat,
1 g saturated fat, 1 g protein, 10 g carbs,
0 g fiber, 6 g sugar, 38 mg sodium

Vegetarian   Gluten Free

Use gluten-free cookies
like Ginger Snaps

Lazy Strawberry Shortcake

Individual strawberry shortcake desserts couldn't be easier with canned biscuits filled with fresh, sweetened strawberries and topped with canned whipped cream for convenience. If you're in a rush and want to skip baking biscuits, look for the ready-made bakery shortcakes that we occasionally spot at Trader Joe's.

1 (16-oz) can Buttermilk Biscuits (8 biscuits)

1 lb fresh strawberries

2 Tbsp sugar

Refrigerated Sweetened Whipped Light Cream (ready-made in dispenser)

1 Slice strawberries and place in a bowl. Stir in sugar and let sit for 30 minutes until strawberries soften and juices are released.

2 Preheat oven to 350° F. While strawberries are softening, bake biscuits per package instructions.

3 Cut biscuits in half, spoon in strawberries and top with whipped cream (about 4 Tbsp). Close biscuit and add more whipped cream on top, if desired. Garnish with a fresh strawberry, if desired.

Prep time: 10 minutes, plus 30 minutes to let strawberries soften
Hands-off-cooking time: 16-18 minutes   **Serves** 8

Nutrition Snapshot
Per serving: 240 calories, 10 g fat, 7 g saturated fat, 4 g protein, 33 g carbs, 1 g fiber, 12 g sugar, 451 mg sodium

10-Minute Lemon Curd

Lemon curd is a thick, sweet-tart lemon spread that can be used on tarts, in cake fillings, or on scones and biscuits. The color is usually pale yellow, and the color and thickness comes from the egg yolks used in the recipe. Some recipes add lemon zest to intensify the color but we love how smooth it is without the addition. Trader Joe's carries jars of lemon curd, but usually seasonally, which means that it disappears for part of the year. As long as you have fresh lemons available, you can make lemon curd any time of year, in about 10 minutes.

½ cup fresh lemon juice

6 Tbsp (¾ stick) unsalted butter, softened at room temperature

1 cup sugar

4 extra-large or jumbo eggs

1 In a 1.5 or 2-quart saucepan (no heat), cream together butter and sugar. Beat in the eggs and lemon juice. Mixture will be lumpy.

2 Place saucepan over low heat and whisk until mixture becomes smooth. Continue to whisk until mixture begins to thicken (about 8-10 minutes). Whisk continuously until mixture is thick and coats a spoon thickly. Do not let mixture boil.

3 Remove from heat. Cool and serve or refrigerate. It will store for up to a week in the refrigerator.

Prep and cooking time: 10 minutes

Makes 2 cups of lemon curd

Nutrition Snapshot

Per tablespoon: 54 calories, 3 g fat, 2 g saturated fat, 1 g protein, 7 g carbs, 0 g fiber, 6 g sugar, 9 mg sodium

Maya Chocolate Fudge

It's so easy to make basic chocolate fudge. All you need is a bag of chocolate chips, some sweetened condensed milk, and about 5 minutes. We captured the warm and rich essence of popular Maya hot cocoa (also called Mexican hot cocoa) in our fudge by adding instant coffee, cinnamon, and cayenne. The fudge is complex and comes with a subtle spicy kick.

1 (12-oz) bag semi-sweet chocolate chips

1 (14-oz) bottle or can sweetened condensed milk

1 Tbsp instant coffee or espresso powder

2 tsp cinnamon

½ tsp cayenne red pepper (decrease to ¼ tsp if you're wary of the heat)

1   Heat condensed milk in a heavy saucepan over medium heat.

2   In a small bowl, dissolve instant coffee in ½ Tbsp water (it will be thick) and stir in cinnamon and cayenne. It will be like a paste. Add coffee mixture to condensed milk and stir. A silicone spatula is most helpful.

3   Add chocolate chips, turn heat to low, and stir until just melted and smooth. Be careful that you don't scorch the chocolate.

4   Pour into a very lightly oiled 8x8-inch pan. Chill in fridge until set, about 2 hours or up to overnight.

Tip: When cutting fudge, a plastic knife works best. Cut fudge when cold and wipe knife clean in between cuts. Then use a spatula to lift out the pieces. You can also line the pan with wax paper for easier removal of fudge.

Prep and cooking time: 10 minutes
Makes 20 pieces

Nutrition Snapshot
Per piece: 154 calories, 6 g fat,
4 g saturated fat, 3 g protein, 22 g carbs,
1 g fiber, 20 g sugar, 20 mg sodium

Raspberry Fool

Raspberry Fool is a classic British dessert that is wickedly simple to make, yet fancy enough to serve to guests. The name "fool" is believed to come from the French word "fouler" which means to mash. No foolin'! Who knew mashed fruit could look so pretty?

1 (6-oz) pkg raspberries, or 1 cup frozen raspberries (half of 12-oz pkg), thawed

2 Tbsp sugar

1 cup heavy whipping cream

1 In a bowl, mix raspberries and sugar. Let sit for 10-15 minutes to give berries a chance to soften.

2 Whip cream until soft peaks form.

3 Mash berries with a fork. Leave some larger lumps for variety.

4 Combine mashed berries and whipped cream, using a rubber spatula to fold. Do not overmix! The beauty in this dessert is seeing the separate colors and textures – white cream, red fruit, and many shades of pink in between.

5 Spoon into serving glasses, garnish with extra berries, and serve immediately. This dessert is best made right before serving.

Prep time: 10 minutes
Hands-off wait time: 10-15 minutes
Makes 4 ½-cup servings

Variation: Wona's kids make a breakfast version using yogurt and raspberries.

Nutrition Snapshot
Per serving: 246 calories, 24 g fat, 12 g saturated fat, 1 g protein,
11 g carbs, 3 g fiber, 8 g sugar, 21 mg sodium

Vegetarian   Gluten Free

Joe-Joe's (Oreo) Milkshake

The Oreo has been the nation's best-selling cookie since it was created in 1912. Who can resist this crunchy chocolate cookie with creamy vanilla filling? We think Trader Joe's made this classic even better, adding real vanilla bean specks for the creamy filling, and leaving out high fructose corn syrup and hydrogenated oils. Bring out your inner kid (and every actual kid in the vicinity) with this yummy milkshake!

1 cup light or regular vanilla ice cream (about 3 scoops)

1 cup milk

5 Joe-Joe's chocolate sandwich cookies, plus more for sprinkling on top

1 Place all ingredients in a blender and blend until smooth.

2 Pour into glasses. Sprinkle additional crushed cookies on top, if desired.

Prep time: 5 minutes
Serves 2

Nutrition Snapshot

Per serving: 334 calories, 12 g fat, 5 g saturated fat, 8 g protein, 47 g carbs, 0 g fiber, 36 g sugar, 220 mg sodium

Use gluten-free
Joe-Joe's

Pear Galette

We love the rustic, freeform appearance of galettes. The best part is you don't need a pie pan, and assembling is truly as easy as pie—pun intended! Don't worry about making the pie perfectly symmetrical. Part of the charm is that the imperfect shape looks deliciously hand-crafted and homemade.

1 frozen pie crust, thawed

4 pears

2 Tbsp brown sugar

Juice and zest of 1 small lemon

2 Tbsp butter

Slivered almonds for garnish (optional)

1 Preheat oven to 400° F.

2 Place pie crust on a baking sheet lined with parchment paper or Silpat sheet.

3 Peel and core pears, then cut in slices ½-inch thick. Toss in a bowl with sugar, lemon juice, and lemon zest. Pour pear filling onto center of pie crust and spread to within 1 ½ inches of pie crust edge.

4 Slice butter into thin slices and scatter evenly over top of filling. Sprinkle almonds on top.

5 Fold edges of pie crust over pears, crimping dough lightly to seal edges.

6 Bake for 20-25 minutes until pears are tender and crust is lightly browned.

Prep time: 15 minutes
Hands-off cooking time: 20-25 minutes
Serves 8

Nutrition Snapshot

Per serving: 277 calories, 16 g fat, 9 g saturated fat, 2 g protein, 33 g carbs, 5 g fiber, 13 g sugar, 42 mg sodium

Vegetarian

Warm Berry Compote

When you're itching for berry pie but don't have pie crust on hand, opt for a compote. Compote (French for "mixture") is a dessert originating from medieval Europe, made of fruit cooked in sugar. You can serve it over pound cake, Angel food cake, or vanilla ice cream. It is also delicious over waffles, French toast, or oatmeal.

1 (12-oz) bag frozen mixed berries
Zest and juice of 1 orange
2 Tbsp sugar or honey

1 Place berries, orange zest, and orange juice in a saucepan and cook over medium heat. Taste for sweetness; sugar may not be necessary. If needed, stir in sugar.

2 Once boiling, reduce heat and continue to cook over medium-low heat for 10 minutes, stirring occasionally.

3 Remove from heat and serve warm.

Prep and cooking time: 10 minutes
Makes 8 ½-cup servings

Nutrition Snapshot

Per serving: 50 calories, 0 g fat, 0 g saturated fat, 1 g protein, 11 g carbs, 3 g fiber, 7 g sugar, 0 mg sodium

Elephant Ears (Palmiers)

Palmiers (pronounced palm-yay) are French cookies that are buttery, crispy, and simply irresistible. They're also called Elephant Ears because, well, they look like elephant ears. They are super easy to make with store-bought puff pastry. Most recipes for palmiers call for 2 cups of sugar, but we found that ½ cup was plenty. We think that Trader Joe's puff pastry, made with real butter, is superior to all other brands. The bad news? It seems to be available only during the fall and winter seasons, so stock up on a few extras and keep frozen.

1 (16-oz) pkg frozen Puff Pastry, thawed
½ cup sugar
1 tsp cinnamon (optional)

1   Preheat oven to 400° F. Line baking sheets with parchment paper or Silpat baking mats.

2   Unfold puff pastry sheets and roll flat to smooth, if needed.

3   Combine sugar and cinnamon. Sprinkle evenly over puff pastry sheets. Press sugar into puff pastry, using a rolling pin to press evenly.

4   Starting with long edges, roll opposite edges of puff pastry toward the center, meeting in the middle. Slice log into 3/8-inch slices and place onto baking sheets.

5   Bake for 10 minutes. Flip palmiers and bake 7 minutes more or until golden brown.

Tip: Thaw puff pastry in the refrigerator. It will be much easier to handle and cut puff pastry when it is cold.

Prep time: 15 minutes
Cooking time: 17 minutes (mostly hands off)
Makes about 40 cookies

Variations: Use ½ cup fruit jam instead of sugar for the filling. Or try Cranberry Butter, Fig Butter, or Pumpkin Butter (and add 2 Tbsp sugar since these are less sweet than fruit jams).

Nutrition Snapshot
Per cookie: 74 calories, 4 g fat, 3 g saturated fat, 1 g protein,
8 g carbs, 0 g fiber, 3 g sugar, 54 mg sodium

Instant Margaritas

When you need a margarita ready in an instant, and we mean INSTANT, try using Trader Joe's freshly squeezed limeade. It's lightly sweetened and tastes very fresh. A crewmember gave us this tip for a truly effortless cocktail.

1 (32-fl-oz) bottle refrigerated Freshly Squeezed Limeade, 4 cups

1 ½ cups tequila

½ cup orange liqueur such as Cointreau or Bols Triple Sec (optional)

Juice from 2 limes, plus wedges or slices for garnish

Salt for rimming glasses (optional)

1 Combine limeade, tequila, orange liqueur, and lime juice. Keep in fridge until ready to serve. If serving right away, add ice and stir.

2 Salt rims of serving glasses. Serve with lime wedges for garnish.

Prep time: 5 minutes
Serves 8

For a single serving:

½ cup Freshly Squeezed Limeade

3 Tbsp tequila

1 Tbsp orange liqueur such as Cointreau or Bols (optional)

Juice from half a lime, plus a wedge or slice for garnish

Salt for rimming glass (optional)

Nutrition Snapshot

*Per serving: 206 calories, 0 g fat, 0 g saturated fat, 0 g protein,
21 g carbs, 0 g fiber, 18 g sugar, 5 mg sodium*

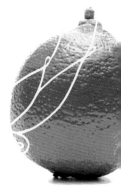

Nice Rice Pudding

Warm rice pudding is a comfort-food dessert that is rarely refused at our house. Creamy, sweet, thick pudding is flavored with vanilla and cinnamon. Top with sliced almonds, jam, or fresh fruit. If pudding gets too thick, add some milk or water to thin it out. This tip also works on leftover rice pudding.

4 cups whole milk

1 cup white rice (use short grain for creamier texture)

¼ cup sugar

Pinch salt

1 tsp vanilla extract

½ tsp cinnamon

1 Place milk, rice, sugar, and salt in a medium saucepan and bring to a boil over medium-high heat, stirring occasionally.

2 Lower heat to a simmer and cook uncovered, stirring occasionally, until rice is tender and mixture thickens, about 20 minutes.

3 Remove from the heat and stir in vanilla and cinnamon.

Prep and cooking time: 30 minutes   **Serves** 8

Nutrition Snapshot

Per serving: 191 calories, 4 g fat, 3 g saturated fat, 6 g protein, 33 g carbs, 0 g fiber, 13 g sugar, 328 mg sodium

Cocoa Almond (Nutella) Crescents

Folks, what we have here is 3-ingredient bliss. Warm soft rolls are filled with banana and smooth Cocoa Almond Spread, Trader Joe's version of Nutella; joy guaranteed in every bite. If you're in a chocolate-only mood, use only Cocoa Almond Spread and skip the fruit. Or try using fresh raspberries instead of banana, 2-3 raspberries per crescent roll.

1 (8-oz) can refrigerated Crescent Rolls
8 tsp Cocoa Almond Spread
1 small banana, cut into 8 chunks

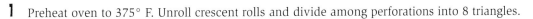

1 Preheat oven to 375° F. Unroll crescent rolls and divide among perforations into 8 triangles.

2 Place 1 tsp cocoa spread near the wider end of each triangle. Top with banana. Roll up and shape into crescents. Place on baking sheet.

3 Bake until golden brown, about 12-14 minutes. Remove from oven and serve immediately.

Prep time: 10 minutes   **Hands-off cooking time:** 12-14 minutes
Makes 8 crescent rolls

Nutrition Snapshot
Per roll: 146 calories, 7 g fat, 3 g saturated fat, 2 g protein,
17 g carbs, 0 g fiber, 7 g sugar, 223 mg sodium

    Eat Cocoa Almond Spread
straight from the jar. Yum!

6 Breakfast

Chia Breakfast Pudding

CH-CH-CH-Chia! Whether you're an ultra-marathoner or an Aztec warrior, there is no better way to fuel up in the morning than with legendary chia seeds. This ancient seed and superfood is high in protein, omega-3 fatty acids, fiber, and vitamins. Like flax seed, chia creates a gel when mixed with liquid. Combine chia with milk, wait until it thickens, and enjoy a pudding-like breakfast dish. We love to flavor ours with honey, cinnamon, and vanilla. Yum!

1 cup 2% or whole milk
¼ cup chia seeds
1 Tbsp honey
½ tsp cinnamon
1 tsp vanilla extract

1 The night before, whisk all ingredients together and let sit for 10 minutes.

2 Whisk again so that chia seeds are evenly distributed. Pour into two serving bowls.

3 Refrigerate overnight and enjoy in the morning.

Prep time: 5 minutes, plus 10 minutes wait time (not including overnight wait time)
Serves 1

Variations: Use almond milk, rice milk, soy milk, or coconut milk. For flavor variation, substitute 2 Tbsp of Spicy Chai Mix or 2 Tbsp Cappucino powder for honey, cinnamon, and vanilla.

Note: Experiment to see if you enjoy this breakfast pudding cold or warm.
To enjoy warm, heat pudding in microwave.

Nutrition Snapshot
Per serving: 535 calories, 25 g fat, 5 g saturated fat, 20 g protein,
74 g carbs, 25 g fiber, 45 g sugar, 101 mg sodium

Pumpkin Blueberry Breakfast Cobbler

Everyone loves blueberry pancakes for breakfast, so why not turn them into individual cobblers? Cobblers take the work out of flipping pancakes and have more personality when served at breakfast or brunch. We used Trader Joe's delicious pumpkin pancake mix, available during the fall season, but regular pancake mix will work as well. Top this warm cobbler with a drizzle of maple syrup, a spoonful of Greek yogurt, or for dessert, a dollop of whipped cream.

1 ¼ cup Pumpkin Pancake and Waffle Mix

1 large egg

¾ cup 2% or whole milk

2 Tbsp melted butter

½ cup frozen blueberries

1 Preheat oven to 375° F.

2 In a medium bowl, whisk together egg, milk, and butter; add pancake mix, stirring to combine. Divide this mixture between six small, lightly-oiled ramekins or oven-safe bowls (¼ cup batter for each).

3 Top each with a tablespoon of blueberries (no need to thaw).

4 Bake for 18-20 minutes until cobblers begin to turn golden on top.

Prep time: 10 minutes
Hands-off cooking time: 18-20 minutes
Serves 6

Variation: Substitute regular or multigrain pancake mix when pumpkin pancake mix is not available.

Nutrition Snapshot
Per serving: 193 calories, 6 g fat, 3 g saturated fat, 4 g protein, 32 g carbs, 2 g fiber, 18 g sugar, 267 mg sodium

Use gluten-free version
of this pancake mix

Pancetta and Asparagus Scramble

Crisp asparagus and salty pancetta perfectly offset moist scrambled eggs. Trader Joe's pancetta is conveniently diced into mini-cubes and is terrific in egg scrambles or omelets. Garlic bread pairs nicely with this Italian-themed creation at brunch.

8 eggs

1 (4-oz) container Cubetti Pancetta (pancetta minicubes)

12 slender stalks asparagus cut into ½-inch lengths

¼ tsp black pepper

¼ cup shredded Parmesan cheese (optional)

1 In a medium bowl, whisk eggs. Set aside.

2 In a skillet or non-stick omelet pan over medium-high heat, add pancetta cubes (no oil necessary) and cook until a little fat has rendered, about 30 seconds. Add asparagus and continue sautéing until pancetta begins to look crisp, about 2-3 minutes.

3 Reduce heat to low and pour eggs into pan. Adjust heat if needed, but cook slowly. Move eggs around until they are just cooked, moist, creamy, and tender. Remove from heat near the end and let residual heat of the pan finish the cooking. Sprinkle with pepper and Parmesan.

Helpful tip: The trick to making moist eggs is to cook them slowly over low or medium heat. Cooking them quickly over high heat is only good for creating a chewy futuristic polymer - it makes eggs rubbery.

Prep and cooking time: 10 minutes
Serves 4

Variation: Few dishes are simpler to make than an egg scramble, and it's a great way to make use of any vegetables or leftovers you have in the fridge or freezer. Add sun-dried tomatoes, olives, and goat cheese, with some fresh basil sprinkled on top. Or scramble up a Mexican version with diced chorizo and red bell pepper, with salsa and cheese added on top.

Nutrition Snapshot

Per serving: 182 calories, 13 g fat, 4 g saturated fat, 14 g protein, 2 g carbs, 1 g fiber, 2 g sugar, 323 mg sodium

Omit pancetta and instead sprinkle with
Crumbled Feta, vegetarian bacon, or
Parmesan to add saltiness and texture.

Toad in a Hole

Toad in a Hole is also known as "egg in bread" in Deana's house. It was one of the first things her kids learned to cook by themselves and is still a household favorite. The recipe requires only two ingredients plus seasonings and butter, and it takes only minutes to make. Serve with fresh fruit or avocado slices. Sprinkle cheese on top if desired.

1 egg
1 slice whole wheat or white bread
½ Tbsp butter
Pinch salt and pepper

1 Using a cup or biscuit cutter, cut a circle in center of bread.

2 In a nonstick pan over medium-high heat, melt butter. Tip pan so butter coats the bottom.

3 Add bread, including the cut-out round placed to the side of the slice. Flip over to coat both sides with butter. Break egg into hole and season with salt and pepper. Cook for one minute.

4 Turn heat to low and flip bread to other side. Cook for 1 minute longer or until egg is cooked as you desire (runny, medium, or fully cooked yolk). Serve the cut-out round on the side and top with jam if desired.

Nutrition Snapshot

Per serving: 253 calories, 13 g fat, 6 g saturated fat, 10 g protein,
24 g carbs, 3 g fiber, 2 g sugar, 377 mg sodium

Vegetarian **G Gluten Free**

Use gluten-free bread

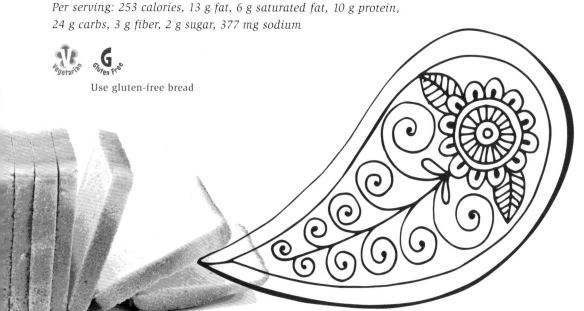

Bacon Cheddar Biscuits

What's better than warm biscuits from the oven? Warm biscuits with bits of bacon and cheddar cheese, that's what. Pancake mix is combined with cold milk and cold butter to make warm, buttery biscuits. We emphasize cold butter and cold milk because this technique makes the biscuits flakier and lighter. You want to cut the butter into the flour and mix until just combined so there are tiny bits of butter throughout coated in flour. Serve these home-style beauties with any breakfast or brunch fare such as eggs, fruit, or country gravy.

2 cups Buttermilk Pancake & Baking Mix
2 Tbsp butter, cold
2 slices Fully Cooked Bacon, crisped in microwave and chopped
½ cup shredded cheddar cheese
¾ cups whole milk, cold

1 Preheat oven to 425° F.

2 Add baking mix to large bowl. Cube cold butter and add to mix, using your fingers to crumble butter into mix until pea-sized crumbles form. Stir in bacon and cheese. Make a well in center of mixture and add milk, stirring only until just combined. Do not overmix.

3 Drop batter (8 large spoonfuls) onto ungreased baking sheet or one lined with a baking liner. Bake for 10 minutes or until golden on top.

Prep time: 5 minutes
Hands-off cooking time: 10 minutes
Makes 8 biscuits

Nutrition Snapshot
Per biscuit: 185 calories, 8 g fat, 4 g saturated fat, 6 g protein, 22 g carbs, 1 g fiber, 4 g sugar, 544 mg sodium

Omit
bacon

Green Eggs and Ham

Do you like green eggs and ham? With our take on this Dr. Seuss classic, you will like them here and you will like them there. By blending the eggs with a handful of kale, we got our bright green color and a nice flavor to boot. We used Canadian bacon, topped it with some avocado, and served it up on a toasted bagel. Please do not eat them in a box or with a fox.

2 eggs

Handful of chopped or baby kale (about ½ cup)

½ Tbsp butter

Pinch salt and pepper

2 slices Canadian bacon

1 bagel (optional)

A few slices of ripe avocado (optional)

1   In a blender, combine eggs and kale, blending until green. You will still see tiny bits of kale in the mixture.

2   Toast bagel.

3   In a nonstick skillet or omelet pan, melt butter over medium-high heat. Warm Canadian bacon in the pan and then place bacon on top of bagel.

4   Add egg mixture to pan and reduce heat to low. Sprinkle with salt and pepper. Move eggs gently around pan, flipping as needed, until cooked. Don't worry if it looks foamy at first.

5   Add eggs to sandwich and top with avocado, adding more pepper if desired.

Prep and cooking time: 10 minutes
Serves 2

Nutrition Snapshot
Per serving: 136 calories, 8 g fat, 3 g saturated fat, 10 g protein, 2 g carbs, 0 g fiber, 1 g sugar, 268 mg sodium

Omit ham or use vegetarian deli meat

Omit bagel or use gluten-free bagel

Fire-Roasted Pepper Frittata

A frittata falls somewhere between a crustless quiche and an open-faced omelet. It's typically made with eggs and cheese, with other add-ins such as veggies, herbs, or meats. In this frittata, we use Trader Joe's Fire Roasted Bell Peppers and Onions along with ready-made pesto for extra flavor.

1 (14-oz) bag frozen Fire Roasted Bell Peppers and Onions

6 eggs

2 Tbsp milk

2 Tbsp refrigerated Genova Pesto

¼ tsp salt

¼ cup Shredded 3 Cheese Blend

1 Preheat oven to 350° F.

2 In a large bowl, whisk together eggs, milk, pesto, and salt. Stir in cheese. Set aside.

3 Heat a 10-inch cast-iron skillet or other oven-safe pan and spray or wipe with oil. Add pepper and onion mixture (no need to thaw first) and cook until heated through. Pour in egg mixture. Use spatula to distribute ingredients evenly. Cook over medium-low heat until edges are beginning to set (about 2 minutes).

4 Transfer pan to oven and bake for 15 minutes or until eggs are cooked through and frittata has puffed up.

Prep time: 5 minutes
Cooking time: 20 minutes (mostly hands off)
Serves 4

Nutrition Snapshot
Per serving: 202 calories, 13 g fat, 4 g saturated fat,
13 g protein, 9 g carbs, 2 g fiber, 6 g sugar,
345 mg sodium

Shortcut Egg Soufflé Muffins

Before naysayers have a chance to argue that this is not a real soufflé, we'll save you the trouble. This is not a real soufflé! The word soufflé comes from the French word *souffler,* which means "to blow up" or "puff up." Julia Child taught America how to make a classic soufflé, which involves whipping egg whites and making a creamy roux base. This cheater's method is so much easier, almost as impressive-looking, and decidedly tasty. Create endless variations – Monterey Jack cheese with peppers and onions; cheddar and bacon; mozzarella and spinach; Gruyère and mushrooms.

8 large eggs

½ cup **2% or whole milk**

½ tsp salt

¼ tsp black pepper

½ **cup chopped broccoli or any other vegetable**

1 cup shredded cheese, any variety

1 Preheat oven to 375° F.

2 In a mixing bowl, whisk eggs, milk, salt, and pepper.

3 Spray four ramekins with olive oil spray. Add broccoli and cheese, filling ramekins halfway. Pour egg mixture into ramekins and fill to top.

4 Place ramekins on baking sheet and bake for 30 minutes until high and fluffy. Serve immediately. Eggs will deflate a bit.

Prep time: 10 minutes
Hands-off cooking time: 30 minutes
Serves 4

Nutrition Snapshot
Per serving: 278 calories, 20 g fat,
8 g saturated fat, 21 g protein, 3 g carbs,
0 g fiber, 3 g sugar, 628 mg sodium

Cottage Cheese Mini Pancakes

These little pancakes are packed with protein and fiber. They may not rival the fluffy texture of traditional pancakes, but they are far superior in nutritional value.

1 cup rolled oats
1 cup lowfat or regular cottage cheese
2 eggs
½ tsp vanilla extract
2 Tbsp water or milk

1 Place rolled oats in a blender and grind oats to make oat flour.

2 Add remaining ingredients to blender and mix until smooth.

3 Drop batter by rounded ¼-cup portions onto greased griddle or skillet. Cook 1-2 minutes per side, until lightly browned.

4 Serve with your favorite pancake fixings.

Prep time: 10 minutes
Cooking time: 10 minutes
Makes 8 3.5-inch mini-pancakes

Nutrition Snapshot

Per mini-pancake: 79 calories, 2 g fat,
1 g saturated fat, 7 g protein, 8 g carbs,
1 g fiber, 1 g sugar, 113 mg sodium

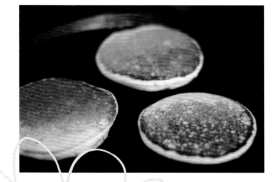

Use oats tested
for gluten

Black Bean Breakfast Bowl

We deconstructed a burrito to create a nutritious breakfast bowl packed with protein and fiber. Taking away the tortilla frees you up to prepare your eggs any way you like. Top with shredded cheese if desired.

1 (15-oz) can black beans, rinsed and drained

2 large eggs

1 tsp oil or butter

¼ cup refrigerated Soy Chorizo

¼ cup refrigerated Roasted Tomatillo Salsa, or your favorite salsa

Half a small avocado

1 Heat beans and chorizo in microwave or saucepan.

2 Lightly grease a pan over medium heat and cook eggs. Pictured here are fried eggs, but you can scramble or prepare eggs any way you wish. We recommend cooking eggs slowly at low temperature.

3 Divide warm beans and chorizo into 2 bowls. Top with eggs. Spoon salsa on top, and finish with slices of avocado.

Prep and cooking time: 10 minutes
Serves 2

Variations: Use pinto beans or lentils as the base. Add leftover vegetables such as spinach, mushrooms, or tomatoes.

Nutrition Snapshot
Per serving: 344 calories, 14 g fat, 3 g saturated fat,
23 g protein, 43 g carbs, 10 g fiber, 3 g sugar, 758 mg sodium

Vegetarian Gluten Free

Greek Egg Scramble

People have been scrambling eggs for centuries. It's the perfect quick meal when you're short on time and ingredients. This Greek-themed egg scramble is a versatile entrée that works for breakfast, lunch, or dinner. Serve with crusty olive bread or toast.

4 eggs

2 cups packed baby spinach, roughly chopped

1 tomato, diced (about ½ cup)

¼ cup reduced fat or regular Crumbled Feta Cheese

1 tsp chopped fresh parsley

½ tsp olive oil

Pinch salt and pepper

1   Whisk eggs, salt, and pepper in a small mixing bowl. Set aside.

2   Heat oil in a skillet over medium heat. Add spinach and cook for 1-2 minutes until spinach is wilted.

3   Add tomatoes and eggs. Reduce heat to medium-low and cook to desired doneness, stirring gently.

4   Sprinkle with feta cheese and parsley.

Prep and cooking time: 10 minutes
Serves 2

Nutrition Snapshot
Per serving: 206 calories, 14 g fat, 4 g saturated fat, 17 g protein, 6 g carbs, 3 g fiber, 3 g sugar, 622 mg sodium

 Vegetarian   Gluten Free

Brioche French Toast

If ever there was a way to make French Toast even more decadent, it's by making it with brioche. Brioche is a French bread made with extra eggs and butter, giving it a buttery rich flavor and tender texture. They are pull-apart buns, but if you don't pull them apart, you can slice the brioche like a loaf. If you're planning ahead, it's best to let the brioche sit for a few days to get partially stale so that it doesn't break as easily when soaked. Serve this delicious French toast with fresh fruit, syrup, or our Warm Berry Compote (page 22). Alternatively, use challah, a sweet braided Jewish bread.

1 (12-oz) loaf brioche or (16-oz) loaf challah

6 eggs

1 ½ cups 2% or whole milk

1 tsp vanilla extract

½ tsp cinnamon

2 tsp vegetable oil or butter

1 Cut brioche into ¾-inch slices. Heat griddle or skillet over medium heat.

2 Whisk eggs, milk, vanilla, and cinnamon in a large shallow bowl. A pie pan works well too.

3 Dip brioche into egg mixture and soak both sides. Let excess drip off. Handle carefully because brioche can be fragile when wet.

4 Lightly grease griddle and cook soaked brioche for 2 minutes per side or until browned. Keep cooked French toast under foil to keep warm while the other pieces are cooking.

Prep and cooking time: 20 minutes
Makes 12 slices

Nutrition Snapshot
Per slice: 180 calories, 10 g fat, 5 g saturated fat, 7 g protein, 16 g carbs, 0 g fiber, 4 g sugar, 214 mg sodium

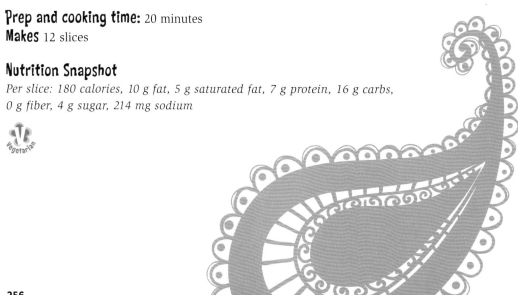

Recipe Index

TJ Store Locations

Alabama

Birmingham - *Opening Oct 2015*
209 Summit Blvd.
Birmingham, AL 35243
Phone: TBD

Arizona

Ahwatukee # 177
4025 E. Chandler Blvd., Ste. 38
Ahwatukee, AZ 85048
Phone: 480-759-2295

Glendale # 085
7720 West Bell Road
Glendale, AZ 85308
Phone: 623-776-7414

Mesa # 089
2050 East Baseline Rd.
Mesa, AZ 85204
Phone: 480-632-0951

Paradise Valley # 282
4726 E. Shea Blvd.
Phoenix, AZ 85028
Phone: 602-485-7788

Phoenix (Town & Country) # 090
4821 N. 20th Street
Phoenix, AZ 85016
Phone: 602-912-9022

Prescott
252 Lee Blvd.
Prescott, AZ 85016
Phone: 602-912-9022

Scottsdale (North) # 087
7555 E. Frank Lloyd Wright
N. Scottsdale, AZ 85260
Phone: 480-367-8920

Scottsdale # 094
6202 N. Scottsdale Road
Scottsdale, AZ 85253
Phone: 480-948-9886

Surprise # 092
14095 West Grand Ave.
Surprise, AZ 85374
Phone: 623-546-1640

Tempe # 093
6460 S. McClintock Drive
Tempe, AZ 85283
Phone: 480-838-4142

Tucson (Crossroads) # 088
4766 East Grant Road
Tucson, AZ 85712
Phone: 520-323-4500

Tucson (Wilmot & Speedway)# 095
1101 N. Wilmot Rd.
Suite #147
Tucson, AZ 85712
Phone: 520-733-1313

Tucson (Campbell & Limberlost) # 191
4209 N. Campbell Ave.
Tucson, AZ 85719
Phone: 520-325-0069

Tucson - Oro Valley # 096
7912 N. Oracle
Oro Valley, AZ 85704
Phone: 520-797-4207

California

Agoura Hills
28941 Canwood Street
Agoura Hills, CA 91301
Phone: 818-865-8217

Alameda # 109
2217 South Shore Center
Alameda, CA 94501
Phone: 510-769-5450

Aliso Viejo # 195
The Commons
26541 Aliso Creek Road
Aliso Viejo, CA 92656
Phone: 949-643-5531

Arroyo Grande # 117
955 Rancho Parkway
Arroyo Grande, CA 93420
Phone: 805-474-6114

Bakersfield # 014
8200-C 21 Stockdale Hwy.
Bakersfield, CA 93311
Phone: 661-837-8863

Berkeley #186
1885 University Ave.
Berkeley, CA 94703
Phone: 510-204-9074

Bixby Knolls # 116
4121 Atlantic Ave.
Bixby Knolls, CA 90807
Phone: 562-988-0695

Brea # 011
2500 E. Imperial Hwy.
Suite 177
Brea, CA 92821
Phone 714-257-1180

Brentwood # 201
5451 Lone Tree Way
Brentwood, CA 94513
Phone: 925-516-3044

Burbank # 124
214 East Alameda
Burbank, CA 91502
Phone: 818-848-4299

Camarillo # 114
363 Carmen Drive
Camarillo, CA 93010
Phone: 805-388-1925

Campbell # 073
1875 Bascom Avenue
Campbell, CA 95008
Phone: 408-369-7823

Capitola # 064
3555 Clares Street #D
Capitola, CA 95010
Phone: 831-464-0115

Carlsbad # 220
2629 Gateway Road
Carlsbad, CA 92009
Phone: 760-603-8473

Castro Valley # 084
22224 Redwood Road
Castro Valley, CA 94546
Phone: 510-538-2738

Cathedral City # 118
67-720 East Palm Cyn.
Cathedral City, CA 92234
Phone: 760-202-0090

Cerritos # 104
12861 Towne Center Drive
Cerritos, CA 90703
Phone: 562-402-5148

Chatsworth # 184
10330 Mason Ave.
Chatsworth, CA 91311
Phone: 818-341-3010

Chico # 199
801 East Ave., Suite #110
Chico, CA 95926
Phone: 530-343-9920

Chino Hills # 216
13911 Peyton Dr.
Chino Hills, CA 91709
Phone: 909-627-1404

Chula Vista # 120
878 Eastlake Parkway,
Suite 810
Chula Vista, CA 91914
Phone: 619-656-5370

Claremont # 214
475 W. Foothill Blvd.
Claremont, CA 91711
Phone: 909-625-8784

Clovis # 180
1077 N. Willow, Suite 101
Clovis, CA 93611
Phone: 559-325-3120

Concord (Oak Grove & Treat) # 083
785 Oak Grove Road
Concord, CA 94518
Phone: 925-521-1134

Concord (Airport) # 060
1150 Concord Ave.
Concord, CA 94520
Phone: 925-689-2990

Corona # 213
2790 Cabot Drive, Ste. 165
Corona, CA 92883
Phone: 951-603-0299

Costa Mesa # 035
640 W. 17th Street
Costa Mesa, CA 92627
Phone: 949-642-5134

Culver City # 036
9290 Culver Blvd.
Culver City, CA 90232
Phone: 310-202-1108

Daly City # 074
417 Westlake Center
Daly City, CA 94015
Phone: 650-755-3825

Danville # 065
85 Railroad Ave.
Danville, CA 94526
Phone: 925-838-5757

Davis # 182
885 Russell Blvd.
Davis, CA 95616
Phone: 530-757-2693

Del Mar / San Diego
13480 Highlands Place
San Diego, CA 92130
Phone: 858-755-7130

Eagle Rock # 055
1566 Colorado Blvd.
Eagle Rock, CA 90041
Phone: 323-257-6422

El Cerrito # 108
225 El Cerrito Plaza
El Cerrito, CA 94530
Phone: 510-524-7609

Elk Grove # 190
9670 Bruceville Road
Elk Grove, CA 95757
Phone: 916-686-9980

Emeryville # 072
5700 Christie Avenue
Emeryville, CA 94608
Phone: 510-658-8091

Encinitas # 025
115 N. El Camino Real, Suite A
Encinitas, CA 92024
Phone: 760-634-2114

Encino # 056
17640 Burbank Blvd.
Encino, CA 91316
Phone: 818-990-7751

Escondido # 105
1885 So. Centre City
Pkwy., Unit "A"
Escondido, CA 92025
Phone: 760-233-4020

Fair Oaks # 071
5309 Sunrise Blvd.
Fair Oaks, CA 95628
Phone: 916-863-1744

Fairfield # 101
1350 Gateway Blvd.,
Suite A1-A7
Fairfield, CA 94533
Phone: 707-434-0144

Folsom # 172
850 East Bidwell
Folsom, CA 95630
Phone: 916-817-8820

Fremont # 077
39324 Argonaut Way
Fremont, CA 94538
Phone: 510-794-1386

Fresno # 008
5376 N. Blackstone
Fresno, CA 93710
Phone: 559-222-4348

Glendale # 053
130 N. Glendale Ave.
Glendale, CA 91206
Phone: 818-637-2990

Goleta # 110
5767 Calle Real
Goleta, CA 93117
Phone: 805-692-2234

Granada Hills # 044
11114 Balboa Blvd.
Granada Hills, CA 91344
Phone: 818-368-6461

Hollywood
1600 N. Vine Street
Los Angeles, CA 90028
Phone: 323-856-0689

Huntington Bch. # 047
18681-101 Main Street
Huntington Bch.,
CA 92648
Phone: 714-848-9640

Huntington Bch. # 241
21431 Brookhurst St.
Huntington Bch.,
CA 92646
Phone: 714-968-4070

Huntington Harbor
Huntington Harbour Mall
16821 Algonquin St.
Huntington Bch., CA 92649
Phone: 714-846-7307

**Irvine (Irvine &
Sand Cyn) # 210**
6222 Irvine Blvd.
Irvine, CA 92620
Phone: 949-551-6402

**Irvine (University
Center) # 111**
4225 Campus Dr.
Irvine, CA 92612
Phone: 949-509-6138

**Irvine (Walnut
Village Center) # 037**
14443 Culver Drive
Irvine, CA 92604
Phone: 949-857-8108

La Cañada # 042
475 Foothill Blvd.
La Canada, CA 91011
Phone: 818-790-6373

La Quinta # 189
46-400 Washington Street
La Quinta, CA 92253
Phone: 760-777-1553

Lafayette # 115
3649 Mt. Diablo Blvd.
Lafayette, CA 94549
Phone: 925-299-9344

Laguna Hills # 039
24321 Avenue De La Carlota
Laguna Hills, CA 92653
Phone: 949-586-8453

Laguna Niguel # 103
32351 Street of the Golden
Lantern
Laguna Niguel, CA 92677
Phone: 949-493-8599

La Jolla # 020
8657 Villa LaJolla
Drive #210
La Jolla, CA 92037
Phone: 858-546-8629

La Mesa # 024
5495 Grossmont Center Dr.
La Mesa, CA 91942
Phone: 619-466-0105

Larkspur # 235
2052 Redwood Hwy
Larkspur, CA 94921
Phone: 415-945-7955

Livermore # 208
1122-A East Stanley Blvd.
Livermore, CA 94550
Phone: 925-243-1947

Long Beach (PCH) # 043
6451 E. Pacific Coast Hwy.
Long Beach, CA 90803
Phone: 562-596-4388

**Long Beach
(Bellflower Blvd.) # 194**
2222 Bellflower Blvd.
Long Beach, CA 90815
Phone: 562-596-2514

Los Altos # 127
2310 Homestead Rd.
Los Altos, CA 94024
Phone: 408-245-1917

**Los Angeles
(3rd & Fairfax)**
W 3rd St & S. Fairfax Ave
Los Angeles, CA 90048
Phone: 323-931-4012

Los Angeles (Burton Way)
8500 Burton Way
Los Angeles, CA 90048
Phone: 310-248-2984

Los Angeles (La Brea)
263 S. La Brea
Los Angeles, CA 90036
Phone: 323-965-1989

**Los Angeles
(Silver Lake) # 017**
2738 Hyperion Ave.
Los Angeles, CA 90027
Phone: 323-665-6774

Los Angeles (Sunset Strip)
8000 Sunset Blvd.
Los Angeles, CA 90046
Phone: 323-822-7663

Los Gatos # 181
15466 Los Gatos Blvd.
Los Gatos, CA 95032
Phone 408-356-2324

Manhattan Beach # 034
1821 Manhattan
Beach. Blvd.
Manhattan Bch., CA 90266
Phone: 310-372-1274

Manhattan Beach # 196
1800 Rosecrans Blvd.
Manhattan Beach, CA 90266
Phone: 310-725-9800

Menlo Park # 069
720 Menlo Avenue
Menlo Park, CA 94025
Phone: 650-323-2134

Millbrae # 170
765 Broadway
Millbrae, CA 94030
Phone: 650-259-9142

Mission Valley
1072 Camino Del Rio North
San Diego, CA 92105
Phone: 619-297-0749

Mission Viejo # 126
25410 Marguerite Parkway
Mission Viejo, CA 92692
Phone: 949-581-5638

Modesto # 009
3250 Dale Road
Modesto, CA 95356
Phone: 209-491-0445

Monrovia # 112
604 W. Huntington Dr.
Monrovia, CA 91016
Phone: 626-358-8884

Monterey # 204
570 Munras Ave., Ste. 20
Monterey, CA 93940
Phone: 831-372-2010

Montrose
2462 Honolulu Ave.
Montrose, CA 91020
Phone: 818-957-3613

Morgan Hill # 202
17035 Laurel Road
Morgan Hill, CA 95037
Phone: 408-778-6409

Mountain View # 081
590 Showers Dr.
Mountain View, CA 94040
Phone: 650-917-1013

Napa # 128
3654 Bel Aire Plaza
Napa, CA 94558
Phone: 707-256-0806

Newbury Park # 243
125 N. Reino Road
Newbury Park, CA
Phone: 805-375-1984

Newport Beach # 125
8086 East Coast Highway
Newport Beach, CA 92657
Phone: 949-494-7404
w

Novato # 198
7514 Redwood Blvd.
Novato, CA 94945
Phone: 415-898-9359

Oakland (Lakeshore)
3250 Lakeshore Ave.
Oakland, CA 94610
Phone: 510-238-9076

Oakland (Rockridge)
5727 College Ave.
Oakland, CA 94618
Phone: 510-923-9428

Oceanside # 22
2570 Vista Way
Oceanside, CA 92054
Phone: 760-433-9994

Orange # 046
2114 N. Tustin St.
Orange, CA 92865
Phone: 714-283-5697

Pacific Grove # 008
1170 Forest Avenue
Pacific Grove, CA 93950
Phone: 831-656-0180

Palm Desert # 003
44-250 Town Center Way,
Suite C6
Palm Desert, CA 92260
Phone: 760-340-2291

Palmdale # 185
39507 10th Street West
Palmdale, CA 93551
Phone: 661-947-2890

Palo Alto # 207
855 El Camino Real
Palo Alto, CA 94301
Phone: 650-327-7018

Pasadena (Hastings Ranch)
467 Rosemead Blvd.
Pasadena, CA 91107
Phone: 626-351-3399

**Pasadena
(S. Arroyo Pkwy.) # 051**
610 S. Arroyo Parkway
Pasadena, CA 91105
Phone: 626-568-9254

Pasadena (S. Lake Ave.)
345 South Lake Ave.
Pasadena, CA 91101
Phone: 626-395-9553

Petaluma # 107
169 North McDowell Blvd.
Petaluma, CA 94954
Phone: 707-769-2782

Pinole # 230
2742 Pinole Valley Rd.
Pinole, CA 94564
Phone: 510-222-3501

Pleasanton # 066
4040 Pimlico #150
Pleasanton, CA 94588
Phone: 925-225-3600

Rancho Cucamonga
6401 Haven Ave.
Rancho Cucamonga,
CA 91737
Phone: 909-476-1410

Rancho Palos Verdes
28901 S. Western Ave. #243
Rancho Palos Verdes,
CA 90275
Phone: 310-832-1241

Rancho Palos Verdes
31176 Hawthorne Blvd.
Rancho Palos Verdes,
CA 90275
Phone: 310-544-1727

Rancho Santa Margarita
30652 Santa Margarita Pkwy.
Suite F102
Rancho Santa Margarita,
CA 92688
Phone: 949-888-3640

Redding # 219
845 Browning St.
Redding, CA 96003
Phone: 530-223-4875

Redlands # 099
552 Orange Street Plaza
Redlands, CA 92374
Phone: 909-798-3888

Redondo Beach # 038
1761 S. Elena Avenue
Redondo Bch., CA 90277
Phone: 310-316-1745

Riverside # 15
6225 Riverside Plaza
Riverside, CA 92506
Phone: 951-682-4684

Roseville # 80
1117 Roseville Square
Roseville, CA 95678
Phone: 916-784-9084

**Sacramento
(Folsom Blvd.) # 175**
5000 Folsom Blvd.
Sacramento, CA 95819
Phone: 916-456-1853

**Sacramento (Fulton
& Marconi) # 070**
2625 Marconi Avenue
Sacramento, CA 95821
Phone: 916-481-8797

San Carlos # 174
1482 El Camino Real
San Carlos, CA 94070
Phone: 650-594-2138

San Clemente # 016
638 Camino DeLosMares,
Sp.#115-G
San Clemente, CA 92673
Phone: 949-240-9996

**San Diego (Carmel
Mtn. Ranch) # 023**
11955 Carmel Mtn.
Rd. #702
San Diego, CA 92128
Phone: 858-673-0526

San Diego (Del Mar)
13480 Highlands Place
San Diego, CA 92130
Phone: 858-755-7130

San Diego (Hillcrest)
1090 University Ste.
G100-107
San Diego, CA 92103
Phone: 619-296-3122

San Diego (Pacific Beach)
1640 Garnet Ave.
San Diego, CA 92109
Phone: 858-272-7235

San Diego (Point Loma)
2401 Truxtun Rd., Ste. 300
San Diego, CA 92106
Phone: 619-758-9272

**San Diego (Scripps Ranch)
221**
9850 Hibert Street
San Diego, CA 92131
Phone: 858-549-9185

San Dimas # 028
856 Arrow Hwy. "C"
Target Center
San Dimas, CA 91773
Phone: 909-305-4757

**San Francisco
(9th Street) # 078**
555 9th Street
San Francisco, CA 94103
Phone: 415-863-1292

**San Francisco
(Masonic Ave.) # 100**
3 Masonic Avenue
San Francisco, CA 94118
Phone: 415-346-9964

San Francisco (Nob Hill)
1095 Hyde St
San Francisco, CA 94109
Phone: 415-292-7665

**San Francisco
(North Beach) # 019**
401 Bay Street
San Francisco, CA 94133
Phone: 415-351-1013

**San Francisco
(Stonestown) # 236**
265 Winston Dr.
San Francisco, CA 94132
Phone: 415-665-1835

San Gabriel # 032
7260 N. Rosemead Blvd.
San Gabriel, CA 91775
Phone: 626-285-5862

San Jose (Bollinger) # 232
7250 Bollinger Rd.
San Jose, CA 95129
Phone: 408-873-7384

San Jose (Coleman Ave.)
635 Coleman Ave.
San Jose, CA 95110
Phone: 408-298-9731

San Jose (Old Almaden)
5353 Almaden Expressway
#J-38
San Jose, CA 95118
Phone: 408-927-9091

San Jose (Westgate West)
5269 Prospect
San Jose, CA 95129
Phone: 408-446-5055

San Luis Obispo # 041
3977 Higuera Street
San Luis Obispo, CA 93401
Phone: 805-783-2780

San Mateo (Grant Street)
1820-22 S. Grant Street
San Mateo, CA 94402
Phone: 650-570-6140

San Mateo (Hillsdale)
45 W Hillsdale Blvd
San Mateo, CA 94403
Phone: 650-286-1509

San Rafael # 061
337 Third Street
San Rafael, CA 94901
Phone: 415-454-9530

Santa Ana # 113
3329 South Bristol Street
Santa Ana, CA 92704
Phone: 714-424-9304

**Santa Barbara
(De La Vina) # 183**
3025 De La Vina
Santa Barbara, CA 93105
Phone: 805-563-7383

**Santa Barbara
(Milpas) # 059**
29 S. Milpas Street
Santa Barbara, CA 93103
Phone: 805-564-7878

Santa Cruz # 193
700 Front Street
Santa Cruz, CA 95060
Phone: 831-425-0140

Santa Maria # 239
1303 S. Bradley Road
Santa Maria, CA 93454
Phone: 805-925-1657

Santa Monica # 006
3212 Pico Blvd.
Santa Monica, CA 90405
Phone: 310-581-0253

**Santa Rosa
(Cleveland Ave.) # 075**
3225 Cleveland Avenue
Santa Rosa, CA 95403
Phone: 707-525-1406

**Santa Rosa
(Santa Rosa Ave.) # 178**
2100 Santa Rosa Ave.
Santa Rosa, CA 95407
Phone: 707-535-0788

Sherman Oaks # 049
14119 Riverside Drive
Sherman Oaks, CA 91423
Phone: 818-789-2771

Simi Valley # 030
2975-A Cochran St.
Simi Valley, CA 93065
Phone: 805-520-3135

South Pasadena # 018
613 Mission Street
South Pasadena, CA 91030
Phone: 626-441-6263

South San Francisco
301 McLellan Dr.
So. San Francisco,
CA 94080
Phone: 650-583-6401

Stockton # 076
6535 Pacific Avenue
Stockton, CA 95207
Phone: 209-951-7597

Studio City #122
11976 Ventura Blvd.
Studio City, CA 91604
Phone: 818-509-0168

Sunnyvale # 068
727 Sunnyvale/
Saratoga Rd.
Sunnyvale, CA 94087
Phone: 408-481-9082

Temecula # 102
40665 Winchester Rd., Bldg.
B, Ste. 4-6
Temecula, CA 92591
Phone: 951-296-9964

Templeton # 211
1111 Rossi Road
Templeton, CA 93465
Phone: 805-434-9562

Thousand Oaks # 196
451 Avenida
De Los Arboles
Thousand Oaks, CA 91360
Phone: 805-492-7107

Toluca Lake # 054
10130 Riverside Drive
Toluca Lake, CA 91602
Phone: 818-762-2787

Torrance (Hawthorne Blvd.)
19720 Hawthorne Blvd.
Torrance, CA 90503
Phone: 310-793-8585

**Torrance (Rolling
Hills Plaza) # 029**
2545 Pacific Coast Highway
Torrance, CA 90505
Phone: 310-326-9520

Tustin # 197
12932 Newport Avenue
Tustin, CA 92780
Phone: 714-669-3752

Valencia # 013
26517 Bouquet Canyon Rd
Santa Clarita, CA 91350
Phone: 661-263-3796

Ventura # 045
1795 S. Victoria Avenue
Ventura, CA 93003
Phone: 805-650-9977

Ventura – Midtown
103 S. Mills Road ,Suite 104
Ventura, CA 93003
Phone: 805-658-2664

Walnut Creek # 123
1372 So. California Blvd.
Walnut Creek, CA 94596
Phone: 925-945-1674

West Hills # 050
6751 Fallbrook Ave.
West Hills, CA 91307
Phone: 818-347-2591

West Hollywood # 173
8611 Santa Monica Blvd.
West Hollywood,
CA 90069
Phone: 310-657-0152

**West Los Angeles
(National Blvd.) # 007**
10850 National Blvd.
West Los Angeles, CA 90064
Phone: 310-470-1917

**West Los Angeles
(S. Sepulveda Blvd.) # 119**
3456 S. Sepulveda Blvd.
West Los Angeles, CA 90034
Phone: 310-836-2458

**West Los Angeles
(Olympic) # 215**
11755 W. Olympic Blvd.
West Los Angeles, CA 90064
Phone: 310-477-5949

Westchester # 033
8645 S. Sepulveda
Westchester, CA 90045
Phone: 310-338-9238

Westlake Village # 058
3835 E. Thousand Oaks Blvd.
Westlake Village, CA 91362
Phone: 805-494-5040

Westwood # 234
1000 Glendon Avenue
Los Angeles, CA 90024
Phone: 310-824-1495

Whittier # 048
15025 E. Whittier Blvd.
Whittier, CA 90603
Phone: 562-698-1642

Woodland Hills # 209
21054 Clarendon St.
Woodland Hills, CA 91364
Phone: 818-712-9475

Yorba Linda # 176
19655 Yorba Linda Blvd.
Yorba Linda, CA 92886
Phone: 714-970-0116

Colorado
Boulder
1906 28th St
Boulder, CO 80301
Phone: 303-443-0160

Colorado Springs
5342 N. Nevada Ave
Colorado Springs, CO 80918
Phone: 719-264-0123

Denver (7th & Logan)
661 Logan St
Denver, CO 80203
Phone: 303-318-7112

**Denver (8th & Colorado)
Grocery**
750 N Colorado Blvd
Denver, CO 80206
Phone: 303-321-1003

**Denver (8th & Colorado)
Wine & Spirits**
790 N Colorado Blvd
Denver, CO 80206
Phone: 303-321-3245

Fort Collins
3500 S College Ave, Ste 110
Fort Collins, CO 80525
Phone: 970-223-3560

Greenwood Village
5910 S University Blvd
Greenwood Village,
CO 80121
Phone: 303-730-3848

Connecticut
Danbury # 525
113 Mill Plain Rd.
Danbury, CT 06811
Phone: 203-739-0098

Darien # 522
436 Boston Post Rd.
Darien, CT 06820
Phone: 203-656-1414

Fairfield # 523
2258 Black Rock Turnpike
Fairfield, CT 06825
Phone: 203-330-8301

Orange # 524
560 Boston Post Road
Orange, CT 06477
Phone: 203-795-5505

Stamford
1041 High Ridge Rd
Stamford, CT 06905
Phone: 203-321-8440

West Hartford # 526
1489 New Britain Ave.
West Hartford, CT 06110
Phone: 860-561-4771

Westport # 521
400 Post Road East
Westport, CT 06880
Phone: 203-226-8966

Delaware
Wilmington # 536
5605 Concord Pike
Wilmington, DE 19803
Phone: 302-478-8494

District
of Columbia
Washington 25th St # 653
1101 25th Street NW
Washington, DC 20037
Phone: 202-296-1921

Washington 14th St
1914 14th St NW
Washington, DC 20009
Phone: 202-986-1591

Florida
Boca Raton
855 S Federal Hwy
Boca Raton, FL 33432
Phone: 561-338-5031

Davie
2296 S University Dr
Davie, FL 33324
Phone: 954-512-2968

Delray Beach
1851 S Federal Hwy #500
Delray Beach, FL 33483
Phone: 561-278-1493

Fort Lauderdale
- *Coming soon!*
1590 N Federal Hwy
Fort Lauderdale, FL 33304
Phone: TBD

Gainesville
3724 SW Archer Rd
Gainesville, FL 32608
Phone: 352-378-9321

Jacksonville Beach
4180 S 3rd St
Jacksonville Beach, FL 32250
Phone: 904-241-1770

Naples
10600 Tamiami Trail N
Naples, FL 34108
Phone: 239-596-5631

Orlando (Dr. Phillips)
8323 W Sand Lake Rd
Orlando, FL 32819
Phone: 407-345-0611

Palm Beach Gardens
2560 PGA Blvd
Palm Beach Gardens,
FL 33410
Phone: 561-514-6455

Pembroke Pines
11960 Pines Blvd
Pembroke Pines, FL 33026
Phone: 954-432-0405

Pinecrest
9205 S Dixie Hwy
Miami, FL 33156
Phone: 305-661-1432

Sarasota
4101 S Tamiami Trail
Sarasota, FL 34231
Phone: 941-922-5727

St Petersburg
2742 4th St N
St Petersburg, FL 33704
Phone: 727-824-0907

Tallahassee
3425 Thomasville Rd
Tallahassee, FL 32309
Phone: 850-894-2538

Tampa
3808 W Swann Ave
Tampa, FL 33609
Phone: 813-872-6846

Wellington
2877 South State Rd
Wellington, FL 33414
Phone: 561-656-1067

Winter Park
131 N Orlando Ave
Winter Park, FL 32789
Phone: 407-622-0874

Georgia
Athens
1850 Epps Bridge Parkway
Athens, GA 30606
Phone: 706-583-8934

Atlanta (Buckhead) # 735
3183 Peachtree Rd NE
Atlanta, GA 30305
Phone: 404-842-0907

Atlanta (Midtown) # 730
931 Monroe Dr., NE
Atlanta, GA 30308
Phone: 404-815-9210

Marietta # 732
4250 Roswell Road
Marietta, GA 30062
Phone: 678-560-3585

Norcross # 734
5185 Peachtree Parkway,
Bld. 1200
Norcross, GA 30092
Phone: 678-966-9236

Roswell # 733
635 W. Crossville Road
Roswell, GA 30075
Phone: 770-645-8505

Sandy Springs # 731
6277 Roswell Road NE
Sandy Springs, GA 30328
Phone: 404-236-2414

Idaho
Boise
300 S Capitol Blvd
Boise, ID 83702
Phone: 208-336-7282

Illinois
Algonquin # 699
1800 South Randall Road
Algonquin, IL 60102
Phone: 847-854-4886

Arlington Heights # 687
17 W. Rand Road
Arlington Heights,IL 60004
Phone: 847-506-0752

Batavia # 689
1942 West Fabyan
Parkway #222
Batavia, IL 60510
Phone: 630-879-3234

Chicago (River North)
44 E. Ontario St.
Chicago, IL 60611
Phone: 312-951-6369

Chicago (Lincoln & Grace)
3745 North Lincoln Ave.
Chicago, IL 60613
Phone: 773-248-4920

Chicago (Lincoln Park)
1840 North Clybourn
Avenue #200
Chicago, IL 60614
Phone: 312-274-9733

Chicago (South Loop)
1147 S. Wabash Ave.
Chicago, IL 60605
Phone: 312-588-0489

Chicago (Diversey Pkwy)
667 W. Diversey Pkwy
Chicago, IL 60614
Phone: 773-935-7255

Downers Grove # 683
122 Ogden Ave.
Downers Grove, IL 60515
Phone: 630-241-1662

Evanston
1211 Chicago Ave
Evanston, IL 60202
Phone: 847-733-0690

Glen Ellyn # 680
680 Roosevelt Rd.
Glen Ellyn, IL 60137
Phone: 630-858-5077

Glenview # 681
1407 Waukegan Road
Glenview, IL 60025
Phone: 847-657-7821

La Grange # 685
25 North La Grange Road
La Grange, IL 60525
Phone: 708-579-0838
Lake Zurich # 684
735 W. Route 22
Lake Zurich, IL 60047
Phone: 847-550-7827

Libertyville
1600 S Milwaukee Ave
Libertyville, IL 60048
Phone: 847-680-1739

Naperville # 690
44 West Gartner Road
Naperville, IL 60540
Phone: 630-355-4389

Northbrook # 682
127 Skokie Blvd.
Northbrook, IL 60062
Phone: 847-498-9076

Oak Park # 697
483 N. Harlem Ave.
Oak Park, IL 60301
Phone: 708-386-1169

Orland Park # 686
14924 S. La Grange Road
Orland Park, IL 60462
Phone: 708-349-9021

Park Ridge # 698
190 North Northwest
Highway
Park Ridge, IL 60068
Phone: 847-292-1108

Schaumburg
1426 E Golf Rd
Schaumburg, IL 60173
Phone: 847-619-0095

Indiana
**Indianapolis
(Castleton) # 671**
5473 East 82nd Street
Indianapolis, IN 46250
Phone: 317-595-8950

Indianapolis (West 86th)
2902 West 86th Street
Indianapolis, IN 46268
Phone: 317-337-1880

Iowa
West Des Moines
6305 Mills Civic Parkway
West Des Moines,
IA 50266
Phone: 515-225-3820

Kansas
Leawood # 703
4201 W 119th Street
Leawood, KS 66209
Phone: 913-327-7209

Kentucky
Louisville Grocery
4600 Shelbyville Rd #111
Louisville, KY 40207
Phone: 502-895-1361

Louisville Wine
4600 Shelbyville Rd #112
Louisville, KY 40207
Phone: 502-895-7872

Lexington Grocery
2326 Nicolasville Rd
Lexington, KY 40503
Phone: 859-313-5030

Lexington Wine & Spirits
2320 Nicolasville Rd
Lexington, KY 40503
Phone: 859-277-0144

Louisiana
Baton Rouge
3535 Perkins Rd
Baton Rouge, LA 70808
Phone: 225-382-0588

Maine
Portland
87 Marginal Way
Portland, ME 04101
Phone: 207-699-3799

Maryland
Annapolis # 650
160 F Jennifer Road
Annapolis, MD 21401
Phone: 410-573-0505

Bethesda # 645
6831 Wisconsin Avenue
Bethesda, MD 20815
Phone: 301-907-0982

Columbia # 658
6610 Marie Curie Dr.
(Int. of 175 & 108)
Elkridge, MD 21075
Phone: 410-953-8139

Gaithersburg # 648
18270 Contour Rd.
Gaithersburg, MD 20877
Phone: 301-947-5953

Pikesville # 655
1809 Reisterstown Road,
Suite #121
Pikesville, MD 21208
Phone: 410-484-8373

Rockville # 642
12268-H Rockville Pike
Rockville, MD 20852
Phone: 301-468-6656

Silver Spring # 652
10741 Columbia Pike
Silver Spring, MD 20901
Phone: 301-681-1675

Towson # 649
1 E. Joppa Rd.
Towson, MD 21286
Phone: 410-296-9851

Massachusetts
Acton # 511
145 Great Road
Acton, MA 01720
Phone: 978-266-8908

Arlington # 505
1427 Massachusetts Ave.
Arlington, MA 02476
Phone: 781-646-9138

Boston #510
899 Boylston Street
Boston, MA 02115
Phone: 617-262-6505

Brookline # 501
1317 Beacon Street
Brookline, MA 02446
Phone: 617-278-9997

Burlington # 515
51 Middlesex Turnpike
Burlington, MA 01803
Phone: 781-273-2310

Cambridge
748 Memorial Drive
Cambridge, MA 02139
Phone: 617-491-8582

**Cambridge
(Fresh Pond) # 517**
211 Alewife Brook Pkwy
Cambridge, MA 02138
Phone: 617-498-3201

Foxborough/Patriot Place
350 Patriot Place
Foxborough, MA 02035
Phone: 508-543-1978

Framingham # 503
659 Worcester Road
Framingham, MA 01701
Phone: 508-935-2931

Hadley # 512
375 Russell Street
Hadley, MA 01035
Phone: 413-587-3260

Hanover # 513
1775 Washington Street
Hanover, MA 02339
Phone: 781-826-5389

Hingham
5 Essington Dr
Hingham, MA 02043
Phone: 781-740-2038

Hyannis # 514
Christmas Tree Promenade
655 Route 132, Unit 4-A
Hyannis, MA 02601
Phone: 508-790-3008

Needham Hts # 504
958 Highland Avenue
Needham Hts, MA 02494
Phone: 781-449-6993

Peabody # 516
300 Andover Street, Suite 15
Peabody, MA 01960
Phone: 978-977-5316

Saugus # 506
358 Broadway, Unit B
(Shops @ Saugus, Rte. 1)
Saugus, MA 01906
Phone: 781-231-0369

Shrewsbury # 508
77 Boston Turnpike
Shrewsbury, MA 01545
Phone: 508-755-9560

West Newton # 509
1121 Washington St.
West Newton, MA 02465
Phone: 617-244-1620

Michigan
Ann Arbor # 678
2398 East Stadium Blvd.
Ann Arbor, MI 48104
Phone: 734-975-2455

Bloomfield Hills
6536 Telegraph Rd
Bloomfield Hills, MI 48301
Phone: 248-855-2283

Grand Rapids
3684 28t St SE
Grand Rapids, MI 59412
Phone: 616-977-1819

Grosse Pointe # 665
17028 Kercheval Ave.
Grosse Pointe, MI 48230
Phone: 313-640-7794

Northville # 667
20490 Haggerty Road
Northville, MI 48167
Phone: 734-464-3675

Rochester Hills # 668
3044 Walton Blvd.
Rochester Hills, MI 48309
Phone: 248-375-2190

Royal Oak # 674
27880 Woodward Ave.
Royal Oak, MI 48067
Phone: 248-582-9002

Minnesota
Bloomington
4270 W 78th St
Bloomington, MN 55435
Phone: 952-835-8640

Maple Grove # 713
12105 Elm Creek Blvd. N.
Maple Grove, MN 55369
Phone: 763-315-1739

Minnetonka # 714
11220 Wayzata Blvd
Minnetonka, MN 55305
Phone: 952-417-9080

Rochester
1200 16th St. SW
Rochester, NY 55902
Phone: 952-417-9080

Shoreview
1041 Red Fox Rd
Shoreview, MN 55126
Phone: 651-765-1398

St. Louis Park # 710
4500 Excelsior Blvd.
St. Louis Park, MN 55416
Phone: 952-285-1053

St. Paul # 716
484 Lexington Parkway S.
St. Paul, MN 55116
Phone: 651-698-3119

Woodbury # 715
8960 Hudson Road
Woodbury, MN 55125
Phone: 651-735-0269

Missouri
Brentwood # 792
48 Brentwood
Promenade Court
Brentwood, MO 63144
Phone: 314-963-0253

Chesterfield # 693
1679 Clarkson Road
Chesterfield, MO 63017
Phone: 636-536-7846

Creve Coeur # 694
11505 Olive Blvd.
Creve Coeur, MO 63141
Phone: 314-569-0427

Des Peres # 695
13343 Manchester Rd.
Des Peres, MO 63131
Phone: 314-984-5051

Kansas City
8600 Ward Parkway
Kansas City, MO 64114
Phone: 816-333-5322

Nebraska
Lincoln
3120 Pine Lake Road,
Suite R
Lincoln, NE 68516
Phone: 402-328-0120

Omaha # 714
10305 Pacific St.
Omaha, NE 68114
Phone: 402-391-3698

Nevada
Anthem # 280
10345 South Eastern Ave.
Henderson, NV 89052
Phone: 702-407-8673

Carson City # 281
3790 US Highway 395 S, Suite 401
Carson City, NV 89705
Phone: 775-267-2486

Henderson # 097
2716 North Green Valley
Parkway
Henderson, NV 89014
Phone: 702-433-6773

Las Vegas (Decatur Blvd.)
2101 S. Decatur Blvd., Suite 25
Las Vegas, NV 89102
Phone: 702-367-0227

Las Vegas (Summerlin)
7575 West Washington,
Suite 117
Las Vegas, NV 89128
Phone: 702-242-8240

**Las Vegas
(Summerlin West)**
2315 Summa Dr Ste 100
Las Vegas, NV 89135
Phone: 702-242-0597

Reno # 082
5035 S. McCarran Blvd.
Reno, NV 89502
Phone: 775-826-1621

New Hampshire
Nashua
262 Daniel Webster Hwy
Nashua, NH 03060
Phone: 603-888-5460

Newington (Portsmouth)
45 Grosling Rd
Newington, NH 03801
Phone: 603-431-2654

New Jersey
Clifton
259 Allwood Rd
Clifton, NJ 07012
Phone: 973-777-5020

Edgewater # 606
715 River Road
Edgewater, NJ 07020
Phone: 201-945-5932

Florham Park # 604
186 Columbia Turnpike
Florham Park, NJ 07932
Phone: 973-514-1511

Marlton # 631
300 P Route 73 South
Marlton, NJ 08053
Phone: 856-988-3323

Millburn # 609
187 Millburn Ave.
Millburn, NJ 07041
Phone: 973-218-0912

Paramus # 605
404 Rt. 17 North
Paramus, NJ 07652
Phone: 201-265-9624

Princeton # 607
3528 US 1
(Brunswick Pike)
Princeton, NJ 08540
Phone: 609-897-0581

Shrewsbury
1031 Broad St.
Shrewsbury, NJ 07702
Phone: 732-389-2535

Wayne # 632
1172 Hamburg Turnpike
Wayne, NJ 07470
Phone: 973-692-0050

Westfield # 601
155 Elm St.
Westfield, NJ 07090
Phone: 908-301-0910

Westwood # 602
20 Irvington Street
Westwood, NJ 07675
Phone: 201-263-0134

New Mexico
Albuquerque # 166
8928 Holly Ave. NE
Albuquerque, NM 87122
Phone: 505-796-0311

Albuquerque (Uptown)
2200 Uptown Loop NE
Albuquerque, NM 87110
Phone: 505-883-3662

Santa Fe # 165
530 W. Cordova Road
Santa Fe, NM 87505
Phone: 505-995-8145

New York
Amherst
1565 Niagara Falls Blvd
Buffalo, NY 14228
Phone: 716-833-4687

Brooklyn # 558
130 Court St
Brooklyn, NY 11201
Phone: 718-246-8460

Colonie (Albany)
79 Wolf Rd
Colonie, NY 12205
Phone: 518-482-4538

Commack # 551
5010 Jericho Turnpike
Commack, NY 11725
Phone: 631-493-9210

Hartsdale # 533
215 North Central Avenue
Hartsdale, NY 10530
Phone: 914-997-1960

Hewlett # 554
1280 West Broadway
Hewlett, NY 11557
Phone: 516-569-7191

Lake Grove # 556
137 Alexander Ave.
Lake Grove, NY 11755
Phone: 631-863-2477

Larchmont # 532
1260 Boston Post Road
Larchmont, NY 10538
Phone: 914-833-9110

Merrick # 553
1714 Merrick Road
Merrick, NY 11566
Phone: 516-771-1012

New York (72nd & Broadway) # 542
2075 Broadway
New York, NY 10023
Phone: 212-799-0028

New York (Chelsea) # 543
675 6th Ave
New York, NY 10010
Phone: 212-255-2106

New York (Union Square Grocery) # 540
142 E. 14th St.
New York, NY 10003
Phone: 212-529-4612

New York (Union Square Wine) # 541
138 E. 14th St.
New York, NY 10003
Phone: 212-529-6326

Oceanside # 552
3418 Long Beach Rd.
Oceanside, NY 11572
Phone: 516-536-9163

Plainview # 555
425 S. Oyster Bay Rd.
Plainview, NY 11803
Phone: 516-933-6900

Queens # 557
90-30 Metropolitan Ave.
Queens, NY 11374
Phone: 718-275-1791

Rochester
3349 Monroe Ave
Rochester, NY 14618
Phone: 585-248-5011

Scarsdale # 531
727 White Plains Rd.
Scarsdale, NY 10583
Phone: 914-472-2988

Staten Island
2385 Richmond Ave
Staten Island, NY 10314
Phone: 718-370-1085

Syracuse (DeWitt)
3422 Erie Blvd E
Syracuse, NY 13214
Phone: 315-446-1629

Westbury
900 Old Country Rd
Garden City, NY 11530
Phone: 516-794-0174

North Carolina
Asheville
120 Merrimon Ave
Asheville, NC 28801
Phone: 828-232-5078

Cary # 741
1393 Kildaire Farms Rd.
Cary, NC 27511
Phone: 919-465-5984

Chapel Hill # 745
1800 E. Franklin St.
Chapel Hill, NC 27514
Phone: 919-918-7871

Charlotte (Midtown)
1133 Metropolitan Ave.,
Ste. 100
Charlotte, NC 28204
Phone: 704-334-0737

Charlotte (North) # 743
1820 East Arbors Dr.
(corner of W. Mallard Creek
Church Rd. &
Senator Royall Dr.)
Charlotte, NC 28262
Phone: 704-688-9578

Charlotte (South) # 742
6418 Rea Rd.
Charlotte, NC 28277
Phone: 704-543-5249

Raleigh # 746
3000 Wake Forest Rd.
Raleigh, NC 27609
Phone: 919-981-7422

Wilmington
1437 S College Rd
Wilmington, NC 28403
Phone: 910-395-5173

Winston-Salem
252 S Stratford Rd
Winston Salem, NC 27103
Phone: 336-721-1744

Ohio
Cincinnati # 669
7788 Montgomery Road
Cincinnati, OH 45236
Phone: 513-984-3452

Columbus # 679
3888 Townsfair Way
Columbus, OH 43219
Phone: 614-473-0794

Dublin # 672
6355 Sawmill Road
Dublin, OH 43017
Phone: 614-793-8505

Kettering # 673
328 East Stroop Road
Kettering, OH 45429
Phone: 937-294-5411

Westlake # 677
175 Market Street
Westlake, OH 44145
Phone: 440-250-1592

Woodmere # 676
28809 Chagrin Blvd.
Woodmere, OH 44122
Phone: 216-360-9320

Oregon
Beaverton # 141
11753 S. W. Beaverton
Hillsdale Hwy.
Beaverton, OR 97005
Phone: 503-626-3794

Bend # 150
63455 North
Highway 97, Ste. 4
Bend, OR 97701
Phone: 541-312-4198

Clackamas # 152
9345 SE 82nd Ave
(across from Home Depot)
Happy Valley, OR 97086
Phone: 503-771-6300

Corvallis # 154
1550 NW 9th Street
Corvallis, OR 97330
Phone: 541-753-0048

Eugene # 145
85 Oakway Center
Eugene, OR 97401
Phone: 541-485-1744

Hillsboro # 149
2285 NW 185th Ave.
Hillsboro, OR 97124
Phone: 503-645-8321

Lake Oswego # 142
15391 S. W. Bangy Rd.
Lake Oswego, OR 97035
Phone: 503-639-3238

Medford
55 Rossanley Dr
Medford, OR 97501
Phone: 541-608-4993

Portland (SE) # 143
4715 S. E. 39th Avenue
Portland, OR 97202
Phone: 503-777-1601

Portland (NW) # 146
2122 N.W. Glisan
Portland, OR 97210
Phone: 971-544-0788

Portland (Hollywood)
4121 N.E. Halsey St.
Portland, OR 97213
Phone: 503-284-1694

Salem
4450 Commercial St.,
Suite 100
Salem, OR 97302
Phone: 503-378-9042

Pennsylvania
Ardmore # 635
112 Coulter Avenue
Ardmore, PA 19003
Phone: 610-658-0645

Jenkintown # 633
933 Old York Road
Jenkintown, PA 19046
Phone: 215-885-524

Media # 637
12 East State Street
Media, PA 19063
Phone: 610-891-2752

North Wales # 639
1430 Bethlehem Pike
(corner SR 309 & SR 63)
North Wales, PA 19454
Phone: 215-646-5870

Philadelphia # 634
2121 Market Street
Philadelphia, PA 19103
Phone: 215-569-9282

Pittsburgh # 638
6343 Penn Ave.
Pittsburgh, PA 15206
Phone: 412-363-5748

Pittsburgh
1600 Washington Road
Pittsburgh, PA 15228
Phone: 412-835-2212

Pittsburgh (North Hills)
9020 Covenant Ave
Pittsburgh, PA 15237
Phone: 412-366-1131

State College
243 Patriot Lane
State College, PA 16803
Phone: 814-234-2224

Wayne # 632
171 East Swedesford Rd.
Wayne, PA 19087
Phone: 610-225-0925

Rhode Island
Warwick # 518
1000 Bald Hill Rd
Warwick, RI 02886
Phone: 401-821-5368

South Carolina
Columbia
4516 Forest Dr
Columbia, SC 29206
Phone: 803-790-2404

Greenville
59 Woodruff
Industrial Lane
Greenville, SC 29607
Phone: 864-286-0231

Mt. Pleasant
401 Johnnie Dodds Blvd.
Mt. Pleasant, SC 29464
Phone: 843-884-4037

Tennessee
Knoxville
8001 Kingston Pike
Knoxville, TN 37919
Phone: 865-670-4088

Nashville # 664
3909 Hillsboro Pike
Nashville, TN 37215
Phone: 615-297-6560

Texas
Austin (Northwest)
9722 Great Hills Trail
Austin, TX 78759
Phone: 512-241-1248

Austin (Seaholm)
211 Walter Seaholm Dr
Austin, TX 78701
Phone: 512-474-2263

Austin (Rollingswood)
2805 Bee Cave Rd
Austin, TX 78746
Phone: 512-306-1032

Dallas (Far North)
- coming soon!
4501 Cole Ave
Dallas, TX 75205
Phone: TBD

Dallas (Knox)
- coming soon!
4501 Cole Ave
Dallas, TX 75205
Phone: TBD

**Dallas
(Lower Greenville)**
2001 Greenville Ave
Dallas, TX 75206
Phone: 469-334-0614

Dallas (Preston Hollow)
7939 Walnut Hill Ln
Dallas, TX 75230
Phone: 214-346-6579

Dallas (West)
5550 W Lovers Ln
Dallas, TX 75209
Phone: 214-366-0205

Fort Worth
2701 S Hulen St
Fort Worth, TX 76107
Phone: 817-922-9107

**Houston
(Alabama Theatre)**
2922 S Shepherd Dr
Houston, TX 77098
Phone: 713-526-4034

Houston (Memorial Ave)
1440 South Voss Rd
Houston, TX 77057
Phone: 713-266-2377

Houston (West) -
- coming soon!
11683 Westheimer Rd
Houston, TX 77077
Phone: TBD

Katy (Cinco Ranch)
2717 Commercial Ctr Blvd
Katy, TX 77494
Phone: 281-392-4200

McKinney
2851 Craig Dr Suite 100
McKinney, TX 75070
Phone: 214-491-1893

Plano
2400 Preston Rd Ste 200
Plano, TX 75093
Phone: 972-312-9538

San Antonio
350 E Basse Rd
San Antonio, TX 78209
Phone: 210-826-1110

**San Antonio
(Sonterra Village)**
403 N Loop 1604 W
San Antonio, TX 78209
Phone: 210-545-3123

Southlake
1492 E Southlake Blvd
Southlake, TX 76092
Phone: 817-251-0360

The Woodlands
10868 Kuykendahl Rd
The Woodlands,
TX 77381
Phone: 281-465-0254

Utah
Cottonwood Heights
6989 S 1300 E
Cottonwood Heights,
UT 84047
Phone: 801-562-3024

Salt Lake City
634 East 400 South
Salt Lake City, UT 84102
Phone: 801-359-2462

Vermont
South Burlington
200 Dorset St
South Burlington,
VT 05403
Phone: 802-658-4500

Virginia
Alexandria # 647
612 N. Saint Asaph Street
Alexandria, VA 22314
Phone: 703-548-0611

Bailey's Crossroads # 644
5847 Leesburg Pike
Bailey's Crossroads,
VA 22041
Phone: 703-379-5883

Centreville # 654
14100 Lee Highway
Centreville, VA 20120
Phone: 703-815-0697

Charlottesville
2025 Bond St
Charlottesville, VA 22901
Phone: 434-974-1466

Charendon
1109 N Highland St
Arlington, VA 22201
Phone: 703-353-8015

Fairfax # 643
9464 Main Street
Fairfax, VA 22031
Phone: 703-764-8550

Falls Church # 641
7514 Leesburg Turnpike
Falls Church, VA 22043
Phone: 703-288-0566

Newport News # 656
12551 Jefferson Ave.,
Suite #179
Newport News, VA 23602
Phone: 757-890-0235

Reston # 646
11958 Killingsworth Ave.
Reston, VA 20194
Phone: 703-689-0865

Richmond (Short Pump)
11331 W Broad St, Ste 161
Glen Allen, VA 23060
Phone: 804-360-4098

Springfield # 651
6394 Springfield Plaza
Springfield, VA 22150
Phone: 703-569-9301

Virginia Beach # 660
503 Hilltop Plaza
Virginia Beach, VA 23454
Phone: 757-422-4840

Williamsburg # 657
5000 Settlers Market Blvd
(corner of Monticello and
Settlers Market)
Williamsburg, VA 23188
Phone: 757-259-2135

Washington
Ballard # 147
4609 14th Avenue NW
Seattle, WA 98107
Phone: 206-783-0498

Bellevue # 131
15400 N. E. 20th Street
Bellevue, WA 98007
Phone: 425-643-6885

Bellingham # 151
2410 James Street
Bellingham, WA 98225
Phone: 360-734-5166

Burien # 133
15868 1st. Avenue South
Burien, WA 98148
Phone: 206-901-9339

Everett # 139
811 S.E. Everett Mall Way
Everett, WA 98208
Phone: 425-513-2210

Federal Way # 134
1758 S. 320th Street
Federal Way, WA 98003
Phone: 253-529-9242

Issaquah # 138
1495 11th Ave. N.W.
Issaquah, WA 98027
Phone: 425-837-8088

Kent
12966 SE Kent-Kangley Rd
Kent, WA 98030
Phone: 253-693-3419

Kirkland # 132
12632 120th Avenue N. E.
Kirkland, WA 98034
Phone: 425-823-1685

Lynnwood # 129
19500 Highway 99,
Suite 100
Lynnwood, WA 98036
Phone: 425-744-1346

Olympia # 156
Olympia West Center
1530 Black Lake Blvd.
Olympia, WA 98502
Phone: 360-352-7440

Redmond # 140
15932 Redmond Way
Redmond, WA 98052
Phone: 425-883-1624

Sammamish
490 228th Ave NE
Sammamish, WA 98074
Phone: 425-836-0837

Seattle (U. District) # 137
4555 Roosevelt Way NE
Seattle, WA 98105
Phone: 206-547-6299

**Seattle (Queen
Anne Hill) # 135**
112 West Galer St.
Seattle, WA 98119
Phone: 206-378-5536

Seattle (Capitol Hill)
1700 Madison St
Seattle, WA 98122
Phone: 206-322-7268

Seattle (West)
4545 Fauntleroy Way SW
Seattle, WA 98116
Phone: 206-913-0013

Shoreline - *coming soon!*
1201 N 175th St
Shoreline, WA 98133
Phone: TBD

Silverdale
9991 Mickelberry Rd
Silverdale, WA 98383
Phone: 360-307-7224

Spokane
2975 E 29th Ave
Spokane, WA 99223
Phone: 509-534-1077

Spokane (North)
- coming soon!
5520 N Division St
Spokane, WA 99208
Phone: TBD

University Place
3800 Bridgeport Way West
University Place,
WA 98466
Phone: 253-460-2672

Vancouver
305 SE Chkalov Dr #B1
Vancouver, WA 98683
Phone: 360-883-9000

Wisconsin
Brookfield
12665 W Bluemound Rd
Brookfield, WI 53005
Phone: 262-784-4806

Glendale # 711
5600 N Port
Washington Rd
Glendale, WI 53217
Phone: 414-962-3382

Madison # 712
1810 Monroe St
Madison, WI 53711
Phone: 608-257-1916

Although we aim to ensure that the store location information contained here is correct, we will not be responsible for any errors or omissions.

Photo Credits

Recipe photography
© Deana Gunn and
Wona Miniati
with exception of pages
125, 196, 207
© Jennifer Drummond

Illustrations and chapter
background art (except 232-233)
by © Carrie Stephens
of FishScraps.Etsy.com

Pg 232 © 123RF

All other photos and
background illustrations
© Shutterstock.com

Other titles in this cookbook series:

Available everywhere books are sold.
Please visit us at

CookTJ.com